Designing your own Simulations

Designing your own Simulations

KEN JONES

Methuen · London and New York

First published in 1985 by
Methuen & Co. Ltd
11 New Fetter Lane, London
EC4P 4EE

Published in the USA by
Methuen & Co.
in association with Methuen, Inc.
29 West 35th Street, New York,
NY 10001

Photoset by Rowland
Phototypesetting Ltd
Bury St Edmunds, Suffolk
and printed in Great Britain
by Richard Clay
(The Chaucer Press) Ltd
Bungay, Suffolk

British Library Cataloguing in
Publication Data
Jones, Ken, 1923–
Designing your own
simulations.
1. Simulation methods
I. Title
001.4'24   T57.62

ISBN 0-416-39540-6
ISBN 0-416-39550-3 Pbk

Library of Congress Cataloging
in Publication Data
Jones, Ken, 1923–
Designing your own
simulations.
Bibliography: p.
Includes index.
1. Simulation games in
education.
2. Education – Simulation
methods.
I. Title
LB1029.S53J65
1985   371.3'97   85-13864

ISBN 0-416-39540-6
ISBN 0-416-39550-3 (pbk)

Contents

Acknowledgements

I would like to acknowledge my gratitude to hundreds of pupils, students and teachers who have, over the years, tried out my simulations and experimented with designing simulations. I am particularly grateful to Monika Meinhold, who has used my simulations at a school in Kiel, West Germany, and who kindly supplied the transcript from tape of her students taking part in 'Property Trial' (reproduced on p. 62).

On a personal note

I wrote my first simulation about twenty years ago, by accident.

At that time I'd never heard of simulations. A publisher had asked me to try my hand at producing kits for 12-year-olds about economics – the economy of the family, the community and the nation. The more I thought about it, the more impossible the task appeared to be. How could the children possibly become interested in the balance of payments, the gross national product, or the budget? Even if I based the work on case studies, I could see nothing to stop the children making paper darts of the documents. The problem, I thought, was not one of education but one of involvement. It was then that I thought of the idea of giving the children roles – the Prime Minister, the Minister of Health, the Minister of Education, and so on – and letting them decide on the division of the national budget. Instead of the kits teaching economics, the material would allow the children to participate in economics. Although I did not know it at the time, I had taken the first step towards creating a simulation.

I then had a second idea – to produce realistic documents. If it was a national situation, there could be one or two cabinet documents. If the family had to decide where to go on holiday, I could produce a list of prices and a brochure and map which showed the location of Dad's favourite golf course and the kids' favourite beach. I produced my first simulation, which was a local controversy about whether there should be a shopping centre or swimming pool, or a combination of the two. Unfortunately, the project fell through. But I had enjoyed writing the materials, and it seemed a good idea to devise activities in which students/pupils could be in charge of events and have an opportunity to develop life skills, and the skills of language and communication. Some forty simulations later I still stick to the same basic ideas.

One problem in writing this book has been that authorship is a very personal activity, and a process which is rarely described. In the literature on simulations there is no shortage of descriptions of the finished product, but very little about how the simulations were written, particularly which options and efforts were rejected, and why. If you look at other people's simulations it is easy to get the impression that the authors started off with an educational aim and then the simulation emerged, neatly and logically, in a flourish of inevitability. It is only when one looks at one's own creative efforts that the waste paper basket comes into view.

When thinking about the process of authorship it is important to remember the waste paper basket. One way is to talk to authors about how they write, and another possibility is to compare the second edition of a simulation with the first. Although I have done both these things, I have still had to rely largely on my own experience and to quote rather more examples of my own simulations than I would have liked. However, since the main aim of this book is to encourage you to have a go at designing your own simulations, you should soon build up your own experiences of simulation design.

The style of this book is informal; I've tried to avoid jargon and theory, and to concentrate on practical examples. However, there is a good deal of educational theory, psychology and philosophy implicit in the methodology, which I've tried to elucidate in the last chapter.

In my view, the special contribution of simulations to educational theory arises because they are characterized by action and behaviour, rather than by the acquisition of facts. They are about verbs rather than nouns. The students become active and powerful participants in the learning process, and this has a very profound effect on both students and teachers.

Although I criticize the 'academic' approach to simulation design, this is not because I have anything against academic disciplines, but because I feel that in this particular case 'academic' methods have hindered rather than helped. Such methods suggest that the best way to design simulations is to go through a prescribed series of sequential steps, rather like assembling a motor car – what I term the 'assembly line' theory. My own instincts and experiences favour an alternative approach – a 'cooking pot' technique, of mixing and tasting and trying to get the blend right rather than following a predetermined sequence of activities.

In this book I use the word 'simulation' in two different ways. One is shorthand for 'the material on which a simulation is based', and in this sense one can say, 'The teacher wrote/ bought/used a simulation'. The second use of 'simulation' refers to what happens when the material is used – namely the event itself, including the thoughts and behaviour of the participants. Using this sense one can say, 'The children participated in a simulation'. The word 'simulation' is not unusual in embracing both the materials and the action. The words 'exercise', 'play' and 'game' also have these two meanings. 'The teacher bought an exercise/play/game' refers to materials, whereas 'The teacher took part in an exercise/play/game' refers to an event.

The book is about how to design your own simulations. You are invited to be an author, not a customer. I hope that before you have completed the first few chapters you will have started to create simulations, either on your own or with one or two colleagues. If you have already written some simulations, then I hope that the ideas and examples in this book will help you to improve your technique. And if you have never thought of getting your pupils or students to design their own simulations, then perhaps this book will open that particular door.

· 1 · Introduction to simulation design

Simple simulations

Simulation design is not the prerogative of adults. In childhood it occurs naturally, spontaneously and frequently. Here is an example.

Imagine two children, aged about 4 years, who have some personal background knowledge of doctors, patients and hospitals. Alone, on one rainy afternoon, they decide, for whatever reason, to take on the functions of doctor and patient. One takes the function of a doctor, the other takes on the function of patient. The doctor has a duty to examine and help the patient, and the patient has a duty to explain where the pain is. Their reality is in their minds, and it is the reality of function. In their minds they are neither children nor adults, since age is irrelevant. What matters is health care. The child with the function of the doctor is not pretending to be a child doctor, nor is the patient concerned with thoughts of childhood. The thoughts are the thoughts of aches and pains and injuries, and the motives are diagnosis, treatment and recovery.

If the doctor says, 'Where does it hurt, can you bend your arm, how did it happen, is it a sharp pain or is it an ache?', this is reality of function. It is not a game, it is not a model, it is not theatre, it is not a guided exercise – it is, as far as function is concerned, the real thing. Their personal knowledge of doctors and aches and pains is sufficient to have a simulated and structured environment – the sick bed, a hospital ward, a road accident – and the activity may last for a large part of the afternoon.

However, if the child who is the doctor is having fun by using an imaginary stethoscope without any idea of what it is for, this is not a simulation, it is play-acting and mimicry. Similarly, if the patient suddenly jumps around and cries, 'No, I'm not hurt at all, I'm just pretending', then this is a sabotaged simulation. Even in this simple example it is not difficult to imagine that the doctor could be annoyed that the other participant in the simulation had abandoned the role of patient and taken on the role of child-clown.

Here is another example from the world of children to show the importance of the thoughts of the participants in deciding whether the activity is a simulation or not. In a primary school, two young children are sitting at either end of a sandpit, having been told by their teacher to 'make a sandcastle'. One child takes a bucket and makes a mound of sand, totally absorbed in the enjoyment of the visual effect of the sand flowing from the bucket and the feel of the grains against the fingers. The actions of the second child are identical to the first, but the thoughts and motives are different. The second child may or may not be enjoying the movement of the sand, but the child's mind is planning ahead, thinking how to build a strong castle, how thick to make the walls, whether to have a moat, where to put a drawbridge. This child is functioning as a military architect. Although a casual observer might say that both children are 'playing', this is a mistaken assessment. Neither child is playing – either in the gaming sense or in the theatrical sense. One is enjoying an aesthetic experience, akin to sculpture, painting, etc., while the other is engaged in a simulation.

For a third example, imagine that two tutors at a teacher-training college are having coffee in the staffroom and are discussing their experiences of taking part in the cross-cultural simulation, 'Bafa Bafa', written by a well-known American author of simulations, Garry Shirts. Participation often leads to authorship, and the tutors explore the idea of writing something similar for their own students. They want a simulation involving different cultures, but less abstract than 'Bafa Bafa'. On the other hand, they do not wish to make the simulation into a reproduction of the ethnic problems within their own community. They hit on the idea of having two groups – the people from the highlands and the people from the lowlands, which they label as the mountain people and the plainspeople.

At this stage there are no documents, nor need any be written. As with the two earlier simulations, the simulation design is simple. Like 'Bafa Bafa', the two groups can be briefed separately about their cultures. Unlike 'Bafa Bafa', in which only a few members of the two groups travel to the other community, all the participants in the simulation could take part in the joint meeting. There might be three periods: (1) the two groups meet separately to discuss their forthcoming meeting; (2) the two groups meet each other; and (3) the groups meet again separately to discuss what happened.

As in the case of the first two simulations, and indeed of all simulations, this one is dominated by function. There is a job to do and a problem to be solved, rather than a play to be acted or a game to be played. The motive is not to 'play' or 'win' or 'score' or 'have fun' or 'act', it is the normal motivation of real life – in which people try to do the best they can in the situation in which they find themselves – discussing, arguing, negotiating, explaining, analysing, questioning, asserting, reporting, interviewing and trying to get on with people.

Simulations, games, role-play and role cards

Many authors regard 'simulations' and 'games' as synonymous; or even if they think these are two different activities (or sets of materials) they often use 'game' rather than 'simulation'. This is confusing in an educational context, where 'game' has its own distinctive connotation. In education there can be genuine games in the classroom, and these are not at all the same as simulations.

To call a simulation a game can cause serious problems outside the classroom as well as inside. For example, at the University of California in Berkeley a course in sociology was introduced which consisted of nothing but simulations. Unfortunately, they were labelled games, and despite the fact that the course was successful from an educational point of view, it had to be discontinued because of opposition from parents, politicians and others who objected to the students 'playing games'.

Many teachers have objections to games in education, but not to simulations. So if a simulation is labelled a game, some teachers might not look at it on the grounds that they are in the business of education, not entertainment.

Another problem with labelling simulations as games concerns competition. Most people regard competition as an important element in games, and perhaps an essential element. But many simulations are co-operative, not competitive.

However, the main areas of difference between games and simulations can undoubtedly be observed in the thoughts and behaviour of the participants. If you compare the behaviour of players in a genuine game – say, 'Monopoly' – with the behaviour of participants in a property-development simulation, you will see that the two activities have little in common apart from the subject matter. 'Monopoly' is dominated by scoring mechanisms, measured by the amount of money and the number of houses and hotels the players possess. The players' thoughts are the thoughts of gaming. They try to acquire more wealth, not because they are greedy, but because the object of the game is to win, and winning is measured by property and money. But in a property-development simulation the motivation is not that of the gaming room. Even if the property development simulation is competitive, and many are not, these are usually person-to-person activities, not the attitude of 'Now it's my turn, I throw the dice, move my counter, increase my property, and now it's your turn'.

One explanation why so many simulations are labelled games is that most published simulations have been produced in the United States, where there is a strong emphasis on scoring mechanisms in many educational activities, in keeping with that aspect of the American educational tradition which favours incremental learning and the step-by-step assessment of what has been learned.

However, it is one thing to write a simulation in which one counts the number of votes in a Parliamentary debate, and quite another for the author to build in external marks – participants get 5 extra marks for successfully raising points of order, and 20 extra marks for introducing a successful amendment. This sort of thing rapidly turns a simulation into a game. Instead of dealing with the issues on their merits, the participants try to score points. Reality of function vanishes, and the participants have become players in a gaming activity.

In Britain and in Europe generally, there is less inclination to build scoring mechanisms into simulations, and therefore there is less cause for confusion between games and simulations.

It is true that in business and in the army the word 'game' is often used instead of 'simulation'. But genuine games do not exist in these fields, except as recreation. Therefore simulations which are labelled 'business games' and 'war games' are less liable to confusion with genuine games. Even so, outsiders easily get the wrong impression about what sort of activity is taking place, and even inside these organizations the activities might be more easily understood if they were labelled simulations.

As well as unnecessary confusion between games and simulations, there is a confusion between simulations and role-play. Although simulations have roles, they do not have play, but are concerned with a job and a function, not a new personality.

The following example shows how a teacher might instigate a genuine role-play session. Words which are inconsistent with the simulation technique are printed in italic.

In this *play* I want John to come out and sit there and *pretend* to be a *friendly* personnel officer, and Sally, in your role, I want you to walk in and *act like* a *nervous* person asking for a job. *I'll help* if either of you gets stuck with your *role-play.* I want *everyone else to keep quiet and watch the performance.*

This is not a simulation because it imparts personalities; it is teacher-guided; and it is episodic. In a simulation the personnel officer would not 'pretend' but would function according to the needs of the job. Friendliness would not be imposed on the personality by the author, and the job applicant would not be told to 'act' or to be nervous. The teacher would not intervene, and there would be no audience of fellow-students. If they were onlookers, they would have roles which would explain their presence – trainee interviewers, management observers, or other applicants for the job. In addition, the simulation requires the author to provide enough of a simulated background to preserve reality of function. In role-play, on the other hand, the participants are often required to invent key facts of the simulated environment, which means that not only are they actors, but they are authors as well. Invention and acting can sometime occur in a simulation, but this is usually confined to non-essential details.

This is not a criticism of role-play, or of informal drama, or of the technique of improvisation. All are valuable educational tools. They are, however, not the same as simulations.

Let us turn from role-play to the word 'role'. By 'role' I usually mean whatever it is one is talking about when answering the questions, 'Who are the participants?' and 'What do they have to do?' Thus the word 'role' must include the concept of function – the job, the duties, the obligations. The role could consist entirely of function (reporter, conservationist, explorer), and might be used for several people; or it could include an identity (name, age, sex), in which case it would be for one person.

When I use 'role' I exclude the problem which the simulation is about, and the environment that exists independently of particular roles. Usually this distinction is quite clear. But 'role card' comes into a different category. By 'role card' I include whatever it is that is written on an instructional card given to people who are about to take part in a simulation, including any details of the problem and the environment.

In some simulations the materials consist of nothing but role cards, and these contain all the information that is needed for the action. Simulations can be designed which use no role cards at all, and where all the information is contained in a written scenario, or in facsimile documents – personal memos, reports, etc.

Role cards are instructions similar to a written scenario or notes for participants. They are part of the briefing, not part of the action. They are not documents which exist within the simulated environment. Facsimile documents, on the other hand, are part of the simulated environment. And whereas role cards are private documents for one participant or one group, facsimile documents can be either private or public.

Briefing		Environment	
Private	Public	Private	Public
Role cards	Scenario and or notes for participants	Facsimiles	Facsimiles

Here is a role card which might be written for a simulation about a proposal to set up a new shopping centre.

You are Pat Smith, the Manager of Baker's Tea Shop in the High Street. It is your job to attend the public meeting about the plans for a new shopping centre in the suburbs. Last year the tea shop made a small profit. You are against the new shopping centre because it might put you out of business.

The same information could be conveyed in a facsimile document, which would be part of the simulated environment:

Dear Pat Smith,

As you know, I've been owner of Baker's Tea Shop for many years and would not like to see it close down. Last year we made a small profit, but I'm afraid that if the new shopping centre is set up this would hit all small shopkeepers in the High Street, including the tea shop. Unfortunately, I am unable to attend the public meeting, so please go to it and put forward our views.

Best wishes,

R. Y. Baker

On the whole I prefer facsimile documents to role cards. In real life we do not have role cards. And in a simulation Pat Smith can take the letter to the meeting and flourish it and quote from it; to flourish a role card is to reduce the reality of function.

In thinking and talking about a simulation it is worth making a conscious effort to choose neutral words – participant, activity, action, behaviour – and to avoid words which have theatrical or gaming connections – game, gaming, play, player, act, actor, and role-play. This is difficult, since the concepts of the game and the theatre are powerful and familiar, and the terminology slips easily off the tongue. But using the wrong words can easily lead to muddle at the typewriter and disaster in the classroom. The wrong words arouse the wrong expectations, and the wrong expectations lead to inappropriate behaviour.

Assembly line or cooking pot?

Having examined some of the differences between simulations and other educational techniques, let us look at two different techniques of simulation authorship.

If you have read any of the academic literature on the subject then you will be familiar with what I call the assembly-line theory of simulation authorship. The theory states that simulations should be written rather in the way a motor-car assembly line operates – with the gradual assembly of one part after another until the sequence of steps is completed and the model has been built.

This sequential theory is usually illustrated by a flow diagram with at least a dozen boxes linked with arrows, but at its simplest the theory could be set out like this:

Even in this simple form there are fundamental objections. Aims and contents are not sequential items; they interact. Aims influence the contents and the contents can modify the aims. Some authors leave their aims vague until the simulation has been completed and tested, and then write the aims so that they match the achievements. Moreover, the actual starting point of the whole mental process need not be an aim, but an idea about the contents.

As more boxes are added to the diagram, more objections can be made on the grounds that it is unrealistic, inappropriate and ridiculous to recommend that an author should complete one mental process before even starting on another mental process. The assembly-line theory is a mistake of category; it deals with things rather than thoughts, documents rather than ideas. Even 'aims', which should be mental targets, appear to refer to the actual words which are eventually printed at the beginning of the organizer's notes, thus giving the impression that they were (a) separate and self-contained, and (b) the first item of a sequence.

The 1979 conference of the International Simulation and Gaming Association (ISAGA), on the theme 'How to build a simulation/game', abounded in sequences. And note also the physical association of the word 'build'. Assembly-line academics tend to use the terminology of the car factory or the building site – blueprint, build, construct, model, plan, architecture, specification – rather than the language of authorship – idea, concept, imagination, invention, intuition, thought.

In one paper at the conference a leading exponent of the sequential approach, Dr R. D. Duke, presented a paper, 'Nine steps to game design', in which the first step was not aims but specifications. Duke, who refers to all simulations as games, wrote, 'Game architects need a blueprint composed of carefully delineated, detailed game specifications. At the outset, they need to conform to a plan providing a clear, concise picture of the product to be created'.

The ingenuity involved in Duke's flow diagram can be illustrated by the fourth step, which involves a 'systems component/game element matrix'. This consists of twelve elements – scenario, pulse, cycle sequence, steps of play, rules, roles, model, decision sequence and linkages, accounting system, indicators, symbology, paraphernalia. Although there is dearth of examples to show what these words mean, Duke defines each element impressively.

> A pulse is an organizational device used to encourage multilogue by forcing players to focus on some shared phenomena. One pulse follows another in sequence (or in complex games, several are simultaneously initiated). Each represents an aspect of the conceptual map. During play of the gaming simulation these pulses become tangible handles which allow players to grasp the problem in detail and enter into and to explore the gestalt of the total problem situation. (Duke, 1979b)

In another paper at the conference, 'Format for the game – logic or intuition?', Duke confesses to a certain amount of tongue in cheek, when he says

> Of course, I'm prepared to defend my nine steps as being carefully thought through and useful. And, of course, I can describe in great length why the first six steps will almost automatically solve Step Seven [Game construction and testing]. . . . But the simple, eloquent truth seems to be that

no matter who describes the problem, sooner or later it boils down to 'Go build the game', at which point the designer is forced to resort to his or her own intuition and/or to the format of some other game that might suggest itself from previous experience. (Duke, 1979a)

Unfortunately, teachers reading the recommendations of academics may think, 'If I have to start by drawing up lists of specifications and blueprints before even thinking what the simulation is about, then I'll watch television instead'.

Another first step with deterrent features is recommended by Ellington, Addinall and Percival in their book *A Handbook of Game Design* (1982), and it is intended to cover any form of game, simulation, case study or exercise. It starts with the question, 'Why do you want to develop a game?' If your answer is, 'For fun, or to make money', then you go along one flow diagram, and if you answer, 'For education or training purposes', then you follow another pathway. Both paths entail research – 'Does a suitable exercise already exist?' – and if the answer is 'yes' then you are side-tracked. The educational and training path is perhaps the more hazardous than the fun and money path as it includes more one-way arrows leading out of the design process. But if negotiated successfully, then the potential author can proceed to the second of four phases, 'Developing the basic idea for the exercise'. As a check list, such items can be very useful, but the trouble starts when they take the form of a flow diagram of sequential steps.

One motive for flow diagrams might be the fear that without a predetermined sequence there would be chaos. Ellington, Addinall and Percival may have had this in mind when they stated that there were two different approaches to design:

The inspirational approach, in which the idea for a game apparently develops quite spontaneously, without the designer really knowing how (or, in many cases, why), and some form of systematic approach, in which the design problem is tackled in a logical systematic way.

But the dichotomy is unconvincing. The inspirational does not have to be inexplicable, or illogical, or irrational, and an author can be systematic without being committed to a fixed sequence of thoughts.

Authors of well-known simulations tend to oppose the sequential theory. The most famous of all simulation authors, Garry Shirts, in an article, 'Ten mistakes commonly made by persons designing educational simulations and games', writes

> The designing process, in my experience, is not sequential at all – new idea 'F' requires an adjustment or rethinking of ideas 'A', 'B', 'C' and 'D'. And such adjustment in turn may suggest changes in idea 'F'. One moves back and forth among ideas . . . much as a performer who keeps a dozen or so plates of china spinning simultaneously on slender poles. (Shirts 1975)

There is a less obvious but perhaps equally damaging objection to the assembly-line theory – that by using the jargon of the construction industry it supports the false notion that the job of an author is to build a model of reality. Both ISAGA and the British-based association SAGSET (Society for the Advancement of Games and Simulations in Education and Training) define a simulation as 'A working representation of reality; it may be an abstracted, simplified or accelerated model of the process'. This defines a category which on the one hand covers a television documentary, an economic formula, or a clockwork mouse, but on the other hand doesn't indicate that simulations, at least those in education, are about participants and the powers and autonomy implicit in their roles.

The definition, like the assembly-line approach, refers to physical things rather than to people. Yet if, after a foreign affairs simulation, the organizer asks the participants to comment on what they did, they say things like, 'I thought we negotiated quite well and came up with one or two good ideas'. They do not say, 'I thought we imitated reality quite well and modelled one or two good representations that were accelerated and abstracted'.

If you look at well-known simulations you will see that some authors do not set out to imitate reality, but aim deliberately to distort or restate it, or use fantasy or fiction to achieve their objectives. Even those authors who design simulations to imitate the workplace usually do not try to reproduce the whole of reality, or even simplify it in the automatic way in which a statistician might use round numbers for large figures. Instead, they use educational criteria, they select those bits of reality they think are the most useful, or the most interesting, or the most important, or the most challenging, or the most likely to encourage interaction among the participants.

Not only is the definition 'representation of reality' inappropriate, but it affects the assessment of what a good simulation is. It follows from the definition that a good simulation is a good imitation of reality, and a simulation which does not represent reality is a bad simulation. This is the criterion of the mirror. It means that educational aims, human values, or even enjoyment, should only occur fortuitously, and must be thrust aside by an author if they interfere with the imitation.

This definition in partnership with the assembly-line approach has probably resulted in more bad simulations than anything else. The end products are often overloaded with data, are complicated, unbalanced or dull, involve passive or part-time roles, and contain misleading instructions and advice to the organizer and participants.

To sum up: three main objections to the assembly-line theory are that it is sequential, that it inhibits effective authorship, and that it lends support to the damaging belief that a simulation should be a model of reality.

A completely different approach to designing simulations is what I call the cooking-pot approach. The analogy is that of a chef who stirs the pot and tastes the mixture, and adds or reduces ingredients.

It is the blend and taste and nourishment that matters. The criteria is plausibility rather than reality, consistency rather than sequence, and interest, challenge and involvement rather than assembly and modelling. The tasting of the dish is a continuing feature, and not the same as 'testing', which is often stuck on the end of a flow diagram. And if the chef is inspired and imaginative, then no one need suppose the result to be inexplicable. It is adequately explained by the experience and the ability of the chef, by the type of dish being prepared, and by the constraints and opportunities of the circumstances.

By adopting the cooking-pot approach, the potential author is not tied down to a fixed starting point. The first idea could be an educational objective, or an idea about the contents. The motive could be curiosity, or a desire to try something new, or an escape from boredom, or the desire for money or fame or promotion. And you don't have to draw up specifications or pass any tests before you begin to design your own simulations.

In designing your own simulations, you don't have to work on your own, without a co-author or even without any help from colleagues. Most academics recommend that you should not work alone since, they claim, it is easier to produce a good simulation if someone shares the authorship. Well, yes and no. If you have a co-author, or work as a group of authors, you certainly have the opportunity to divide up the tasks, to exchange ideas, and so on, but there are also possible disadvantages. You may have to accept compromises, there may be difficulties arranging meetings with your collaborators, and the final result might be a muddle because it was not clear who was supposed to do what. Both good and bad simulations have been designed by individuals and by groups of authors. I don't know of any evidence to suggest that better simulations are produced by co-authorship, and even if there were such evidence it should not affect your own decision, which is best governed by your own personal circumstances.

The next five chapters are about practical issues – about the cooking pot, or, if you prefer it, about plates spinning on slender poles. The examples given contribute toward the final chapter which returns to theoretical questions, seeks an acceptable definition, and links the design and use of simulations with educational philosophy.

· 2 · Getting Started

An easy way in

A difficult starting place for writing your first simulation is a blank sheet of paper. It is easier to start with someone else's event. If you are feeling nervous or apprehensive, then don't try to design a simulation from scratch, but start where another simulation ends. Alter one or two of the features, and continue the action.

You can alter the time. You can tell the participants that they are still in their roles, but that it is one hour/day/week/year later. You can invent the consequences of their previous decision-making. The cabinet/board of directors/sports committee resumes its session on learning the news (which you can write in the form of a document, or announce verbally) that their earlier decision has produced a reaction – an ultimatum, a strike, a request for clarification.

You can alter the format. If there are two sides in the first simulation, you could extend the action beyond the point of decision-making so that each side takes it in turn to report back to their own bosses, or supporters, with the other side taking on this function temporarily. Thus the management negotiating team can report back to the board of directors (formerly the trade unionists), and the trade union negotiators can then report back to a mass meeting (formerly the management side).

You can change the roles. Instead of being explorers who have found safety or death on a hostile planet, the participants become teams of space instructors who give a presentation to space cadets about how to succeed, or how failure happens.

If the existing simulation is about journalists producing a news bulletin for radio or television, and ends with the transmission, then you could extend the event by having a meeting of the editorial staff to consider what changes, if any, they should make to their procedures. It gives you an opportunity to provide letters/phone calls/memos which contain congratulations, suggestions, complaints or actions for libel.

Adding another episode to a simulation is fairly easy. It makes use of existing material and probably involves very little in the way of additional briefing. The episode can last for a few minutes, or for an hour or more, depending on circumstances. If it follows on logically and naturally from the original simulation, it will be easily assimilated by the participants since they will be familiar with their roles and the circumstances. It can be introduced without any fuss or bother, and you won't have the anxiety which can arise if you try to do everything from scratch.

True, you may have to do an on-the-spot improvisation depending on the particular decisions which ended the main simulation, but you will usually be able to foresee the way things are going, particularly if you have run the simulation before. And you could always prepare one or two contingency plans, and perhaps write a few documents in advance and then select the one best fitted to the circumstances. It might be useful to arrange for the main simulation to finish at a natural break, or at the end of a teaching period, which would give you more time to arrange the details of the follow-up simulation. And you are not, of course, prohibited from asking the students how they think the simulation might be extended.

In devising the extension do not try to imitate reality, or to play-act the outcome of a real event, but try to achieve plausibility and consistency. If you introduce one or two new items (generally the fewer the better) which are challenging and provocative, you can't go far wrong. It will give you a feel for simulation authorship. You will not be able to publish the extension of the simulation for copyright reasons, but you may get ideas for writing your own simulations.

Four key questions

Whatever your educational aims might be, and whether you start the design process from scratch or extend an existing simulation, you will have to think about the ingredients. You might find it useful to ask yourself four key questions:

1 What is the problem?
2 Who are the participants?
3 What do they have to do?
4 What do they have to do it with?

These questions are not 'steps'. They can be asked or answered in any order, or can be implied in some overall concept. But they have to be answered in an author's mind, implicitly or explicitly, at some time or another, otherwise the simulation will not get written.

Here is how the questions might be answered in the three imaginary simulations given in chapter 1: the doctor–patient, the military architects, and the mountain/plainspeople.

Doctor–patient

Child A   I went to hospital last year. I was in for six days.
Child B   I've been in hospital four times.
QUESTION 4:   DO IT WITH A KNOWLEDGE OF HOSPITALS.

Child A   Let's pretend we are doctors and nurses
Child B   No, I'll be a doctor and you be a patient.
Child A   Yes, all right.
QUESTION 2:   DOCTOR AND PATIENT

Child B   What are you going to have wrong with you?
Child A   I don't know, I think I will have a bad arm.
Child B   I once broke my arm. I'll be able to do arms.
QUESTION 1:   THE PROBLEM OF A BAD ARM

Child A   So what will happen?
Child B   You come to my hospital, and I look at your bad arm.
Child A   I tell you about it, and you try to make it better.
Child B   This can be the hospital, here.
Child A   So I'll go over there, then I'll come in.
QUESTION 3:   DEAL WITH A BAD ARM

Military architect

Teacher A   We're doing a project on castles.
Teacher B   How's it going?
Teacher A   They were motivated at first, now they're bored.
Teacher B   What do they actually have to do?
Teacher A   Find information on castles, then write it up.
Teacher B   Do you get them to actually design castles?
Teacher A   Wouldn't that be too difficult?
Teacher B   You could let them have a go.
QUESTION 1:   THE PROBLEM OF CASTLE-DESIGN

Teacher A   But they get fed up with writing and drawing.
Teacher B   Let them do it in sand.
QUESTION 4:   DO IT WITH SAND

Teacher A   I've got twenty-one in my class, but only three sand-trays.
Teacher B   You might divide them into teams of seven.
Teacher A   A sort of committee?
Teacher B   If you like you could make one the military leader, another could be responsible for the food, another for the storing of ammunition, and so on.
Teacher A   And one or two could be the military architects.
Teacher B   What sort of castles have they been studying?
Teacher A   Crusader castles, so they can be Crusaders.
QUESTION 2:   CRUSADERS RESPONSIBLE FOR CASTLE-DESIGN

Teacher B   So they would first have to decide on what's important.

Teacher A   Then actually build the castle in the sand-tray.

QUESTION 3:   HAVE TO DEAL WITH DESIGNING AND BUILDING CASTLES

Cross-cultural simulation

Tutor A   The best experience was when I took part in 'Bafa Bafa'.

Tutor B   I also did it on my course, it's really multi-cultural.

Tutor A   Can't we do something similar for our students?

Tutor B   We could have two groups, one group being the visitors.

Tutor A   But keep race out of it; one could be the mountain people.

Tutor B   They could visit the village in the plains.

QUESTION 2:   MOUNTAIN PEOPLE AND PLAINSPEOPLE

Tutor A   We could give each of them a description of who they are and what their social customs are.

Tutor B   We could put it on tape, and get them to practise.

QUESTION 4:   DO IT WITH A BRIEFING ON TAPE

Tutor A   After meeting separately, the two groups come together.

Tutor B   And try to understand each other.

QUESTION 3:   HAVE TO DEAL WITH PEOPLE OF A DIFFERENT CULTURE

Tutor A   They could decide to fight or to trade.

Tutor B   They don't actually fight?

Tutor A   No, they are under orders to be nice to the other group.

Tutor B   But they finally meet in their separate groups.

Tutor A   That's right, then they decide jointly.

Tutor B   Decide on policy. It could be fight, trade or anything.

QUESTION 1:   THE PROBLEMS OF INTERTRIBAL POLITICS AND ECONOMICS

These three imaginary examples show the seemingly haphazard way in which most simulations are designed. The two children answer the fourth question first; the teachers begin with question 1 and go on to question 4, and the tutors start with question 2. But it is not haphazard. Authorship is not sequential construction, but the growth of ideas. One idea gives birth to another. Concepts are stirred around, and earlier ideas become strengthened, rejected or modified. It is unlikely that any of the six people would have been aware of the nature of the questions they were answering; for them it would have been a matter of following through their own ideas.

The example with the children may appear to be nothing more than a bit of role-play, particularly since Child A says, 'Let's pretend we're doctors and nurses.' However, Child B does not use the word pretend, and says 'be' – 'No, I'll *be* a doctor and you *be* a patient.'

In deciding whether it is a simulation which these children are planning or merely a bit of role-play, two facts should be considered: (1) there is no personality change which sometimes occurs in role-play, and (2) the structured environment is sufficiently understood to sustain reality of function. The words 'be a doctor' and 'be a patient' do not imply pretence or mimicry. If a man says 'I'll be mother' it is not an announcement that the man will pretend to be a female; it is simply an offer to pour the tea.

Whether the doctor–patient event is a simulation depends on the thoughts of the participants during the action. In this case it is highly likely that the event would be a simulation since both children decided they knew enough about a 'bad arm' to sustain reality of function. The child who is the doctor functions as a hospital doctor, not a witchdoctor or a miracle worker or a character from science fiction. The patient is also likely to be just as genuine as the specially trained simulation patients who provide their services to doctors in training. The injury is part of the simulated environment; it is the behaviour that is real.

The activity 'Crusader Castles' would almost certainly be a simulation. The problem is clear, the roles are well defined, and the children would probably have sufficient knowledge of castles to ensure that the simulation ran smoothly. One interesting point in this imaginary episode is that the simulation could be regarded not only as rounding off a project on Crusader castles, but also as an assessment of how well the children had understood it. However, a problem which arises quite often with simulations is that they are not very good at concluding activities because they tend to initiate new ones. If the simulation worked well, then the children might say, 'Can we attack each other's castles?', or 'We had animals in our castle, can we now try to build a zoo or a farm?' If you have run many simulations then you will almost certainly have come across several examples of spontaneous suggestions by participants for follow-up activities.

The simulation devised by the two tutors would require the greatest amount of preparation. They would have to think of cultural differences. Perhaps one group could shake their heads when they meant yes, and nod their heads to indicate disagreement.

For the two children, the two teachers and the two tutors, the gradual development of their simulations followed a common-sense path of authorship. Some of the problems dealt with in these imaginary examples – plausibility, roles, key facts, powers, autonomy, action and motivation – come up again and again when one thinks 'What sort of simulation shall I design?'

Ways of answering the questions

The following example is not imaginary. It is part of the transcript of a taped interview I had with a 14-year-old girl in a school in a deprived area of the East End of London. I asked the four questions in their original order, and I give this extract as an example of how the questions can be used to encourage the creation of simulations. The girl knew what a simulation was, having participated in several.

KJ Could you devise a simulation? Not just out of the air, but if you were given a problem? Can you suggest a problem?
Girl I can't think of any.

22 · Designing your own Simulations

KJ Anything that has any element of controversy about it? Anything where there is any disagreement?

Girl Seat belts.

QUESTION 1: SEAT BELTS

KJ Seat belts?

Girl You couldn't do much of a simulation on that, could you?

KJ Well, you could. Of course, it's now the law that you have to wear seat belts, except for people in the back seat. So you've got to say who the people are going to be, are they going to be a committee, or a family . . . ?

Girl You could say they were people who were claustrophobic.

KJ Would they want to be in the car anyway?

Girl No, they would go in the car, but they wouldn't want to feel they were trapped in the car.

KJ So at least some of the people are going to be claustrophobics. But who are the others going to be? I mean if they were all claustrophobics the simulation might last two minutes while they decided that they didn't want to be made to wear selt belts.

Girl You could have two people, one who's been in an accident and has been injured by seat belts, and another who's been in an accident and has been saved by seat belts.

KJ Are they claustrophobics?

Girl No, they are just ordinary people. . . . Ummm. . . . Ummm. . . . Seat-belt manufacturers?

KJ You've got to think of some way in which you are going to get these people together. Where are they going to be? Are they going to be in a hospital, or a committee, or a town council, or inquiry, or whatever? You've got to think of some reason why a seat-belt manufacturer should meet someone who's a claustrophobic, or someone who's been injured or not injured through wearing seat belts.

Girl You could have a television programme which is interviewing or investigating into seat belts, whether or not you should have them.

KJ OK. So now you've got another role.

Girl Yes, an interviewer.

QUESTION 2: CLAUSTROPHOBICS, ROAD-ACCIDENT CASUALTIES, SEAT-BELT MANUFACTURERS AND TELEVISION INTERVIEWER(S)

KJ And the actual action itself? Would it be in two parts, one where you meet separately, and then you meet together? I mean would the first part be discussion about how we are going to do it, and then would the second part be the programme itself?

Girl Yes, you'd have a discussion before. Then the interviewers would work out what questions they wanted to ask, and then it would be put like that into the programme. So it would be more structured like . . . like 'We'll ask you that question and then you come up with an answer,' and then you'll get every point of view in.

QUESTION 3: PLANNING MEETING FOLLOWED BY TELEVISION PROGRAMME

KJ So what materials are we going to have to start working on. Are you going to have role cards?

Girl Yes. And you also give a background to what the two accidents have been. You want them to be talking about them.

KJ What sort of document would this be. Would it be a television document, or would it be a background without being a special document anyway?

Girl You could have all these people coming from different groups, like a group of claustrophobics. They'd be a representative of their group, not just one little person. It would be a document, rather than just being background.

KJ You mean like an official document for that association? It would have a heading on the top, like the Society Against Seat-Belt Injuries, or something?

Girl Yes, you'd have documents like that, which could incorporate the background as well. It needn't be in such detail but you'd get a rough idea of the stand you were supposed to be taking.

QUESTION 4: ROLE CARDS AND FACSIMILE DOCUMENTS

Although I supplied the four questions in the order I gave earlier, the answers did jump around, with previous ideas being modified by later ones. What happened was not step-by-step construction, but idea-by-idea development of a concept.

With groups of teachers I have used three ways of prodding them to provide the outline of viable simulations.

Technique A is simply to ask groups to answer the four questions. They can ask themselves the questions in any order, but for the purpose of group comparisons I ask them to provide written answers in the order given. Each answer can be as long as necessary – a few words, a few sentences. The various groups read out their answers to the others, and a discussion ensues.

Technique B is that the questions must be answered in the specified order – the problem, the roles, the task, the materials – and this is done with several groups in timed stages. After the groups have answered the first question, one person from each group takes the written answer to the next group and remains there. Each group then answers the next question in the light of the answer of the previous group to the previous question. After each question is answered the papers containing the answers move to the next group. The person moving can be the same person each time, or the group can choose another ambassador. With more than three or four groups I arrange the tables in a circuit, and the movement is clockwise. It is, of course, much more difficult to construct a simulation based on someone else's ideas, but the technique is valuable because it helps develop critical faculties, and is quite amusing as well.

Technique C is for the organizer (teacher, tutor) to pick a simulation which the audience (students, conference-goers) are unlikely to know, and to announce (1) the aims of the simulation, and (2) the materials (equipment, information, etc.) which is available to the simulation authors. Each group then has to answer the four questions, and give the simulation a title. With this arrangement, the groups compare their own simulations not only with those of other groups, but also with the published simulation. (It needn't be a published one, it could be one which you thought up on the way to the conference.)

Try this yourself as example of Technique C:

You, the author (or your publisher or your client), want to help the participants to understand that our distant ancestors were not primitive (though noble) savages, but were intelligent, imaginative and sophisticated. Assume that the material available includes books on prehistoric nomads who travelled in bands over arid land and who wrote picture messages on rocks about dangers, pastures, and so on, in order to help other nomadic groups. They had no alphabet; no written language. You can assume that you have access to photographs, film slides, video tapes, and perhaps anthropologists who can give you all the data required. Research is no problem; what matters is to convey in some way or other that so-called primitive people were imaginative and sophisticated.

Using this particular example at teacher's conferences, the teachers designed dozens of different sorts of simulations, good, bad, imaginative, dull, long, short, expensive, cheap, workable, unworkable. In one design the participants were members of a television documentary team who had to produce a programme about prehistoric nomadic tribes. Another example was that there were two groups at a university, the academics who were teaching about prehistoric people, and the administration. The academics had to try to convince the administrators that more resources should be granted for their particular subject. Quite a different approach was adopted by one group which decided that the participants were hobos in prison who were frequently moved from cell to cell and who could write signs in chalk on the walls to communicate with other prisoners.

The published simulation is called 'Talking Rocks' by R. F. Vernon. The participants are groups of nomadic tribespeople who all migrate at one particular time from their camp-site to the next one and try to read the messages left by the other group. The information to be conveyed is handed out by the organizer. It consists of twelve survival messages about time, distance and things. For example, one message might be that there are two ponds one day's walk to the east, the nearest pond containing good water, and the farthest pond containing poisoned water. The different groups draw the messages using pictures only, and no modern symbols. They cannot use skull and crossbones for poison, nor can they write letters e.g. N for north. The poisoned water might be indicated by drawing two ponds, one with sheep around the edges the right way up, and the other with upside-down sheep around the edges.

'Talking Rocks' is an imaginative simulation. It is cheap, and it is certainly worth trying in its published form. The manual deals with the mechanics of running the event, including how to decide whether a group has died, and what to do with dead nomads.

Creating simulations as a classroom activity

There are no fundamental difficulties in the way of this as far as authorship is concerned – the principles of creating ideas for simulations do not change with the age of the authors. Obviously, skills tend to improve with practice, but, as we have seen already, young children are quite capable of creating genuine simulations.

Even if the children are not asked to devise their own simulations they may do so spontaneously having participated in one or two. In one class at a school in a deprived area of London, where I tried out my simulation 'Survival' many years ago, the groups worked during a meal break to devise a simulation about planes crossing the Atlantic, involving points of no return. And at a prestigious private school in London some children on their own initiative tried rewriting 'Survival' to fit in with William Golding's novel *Lord of the Flies*.

There are many ways of encouraging your pupils/students to produce simulations themselves. An easy way in, as suggested earlier, is to start at the point where a simulation ends. Then ask the question 'What might happen next?', which should elicit ideas for a follow-up simulation. Sometimes a document is useful to bridge the two simulations. A report of the council meeting which concluded the first simulation could be the key document in the second simulation – perhaps a news conference.

If, on the other hand, you want them to start designing a simulation from a blank sheet of paper, then you might ask them to provide one-sentence answers to the four key questions. You, or they, could choose the most suitable idea which emerges.

However, simulation designing often sparks off a desire to do some research, and this might cause problems. Suppose, for example, they wanted to produce the simulation devised by the girl in the interview – a television debate on seat belts – then they might wish to discover the proportion of accidents which occur (1) when seat belts are worn and (2) when they are not worn. Finding out the key facts can take time, and so it is best to consider in advance whether you will tell them, 'No, it will take too long to look up the facts, so think of another idea,' or 'Yes, go to the library,' or 'You can start on the documents next week, so see what you can find out before then.'

Probably the reason why more of this is not done in schools, particularly in secondary schools, is that many teachers who have no experience of simulations underestimate the abilities of their children. They judge their students according to individual abilities to respond to classroom teaching. They are often unaware of the abilities of the children in groups and in teacherless situations.

It is, of course, all too easy for teachers to pick up a document from a simulation, and pounce on a 'difficult' word and then declare that the activity would be beyond the range of those particular children. Or a teacher who has never experienced running a simulation may have a hidden fear that the children will take the opportunity to have fun and misbehave generally.

My own experience is that even with 'low achievers' in 'deprived areas' there is a considerable amount of intuitive sagacity among the pupils which comes out when they are on their own, as they are in a simulation, and as they can be when creating a simulation. And I find that I also tend to underestimate what children can achieve in simulations.

An example of this occurred when I introduced a simulation

I had designed for teacher-training to a class of 14-year-olds in the East End of London. The simulation had been published as an appendix to my book *Simulations in Language Teaching* (1982) and was about simulations in an educational context, entitled 'We're Not Going to Use Simulations'. It contained several official documents (in 'officialese') and the crux of the simulation was whether some of the objections to simulations were valid.

I had set the simulation in the fictitious country of Lingua and the action involved teachers Jay, Kay and Ell going to the Ministry of Education to meet Inspectors Ai, Bee and Cee to protest against a regulation which said that teachers in Lingua should use simulations as frequently as possible from the third year onwards. The main arguments given in the role cards of the teachers were that since the school was in a deprived area and classes were large, it was necessary to concentrate on examination subjects, and that any sort of activity in which the teacher was not firmly in charge was likely to end up with fighting. In fact, at the school in Lingua a teacher, Mrs Zed, had introduced an activity called 'Walking the Tightrope' which had resulted in fighting. One question which was not raised in the role cards was whether or not this activity was a simulation; in my view 'Walking the Tightrope' was not a simulation because it lacked reality of function, if only because an audience cannot push tightrope walkers.

I could see two problems about introducing this particular simulation: the obvious one that it would be too difficult (these 14-year-olds had a low boredom point) and the hearing at the Ministry was likely to last for five minutes. The less obvious difficulty was that Jay, Kay and Ell had to pretend that they had no personal experience of simulations, whereas they had already participated in three or four of my own.

The reason why I was brave enough to introduce this simulation was that the earlier ones had gone down reasonably well with this class (mainly 'low achievers'), and because at that time I had been rather discouraged by several teachers in other schools who had examined the documents in some of my prototype simulations and declared them to be too difficult. I

MINISTRY OF EDUCATION

Ministry House, Linguan City
Telephone: (0123) 45678

DEPARTMENT OF APPEAL

Head Teacher,
Blue School,
Linguan City North.

Your reference

Our reference   3012/RE

Date   10th February

Dear Head Teacher,

The Inspectorate Department has passed on to us your Application for Appeal against a Ministerial Decision - namely the last sentence of Article 163 (Page 61) of the Ministry of Education Decision Paper.

The Department of Appeal has decided to allow the Appeal to take place, since the application conforms to Clause 25 (b) of the Appeals Procedure.

The hearing will take place in Room 416 at the above address on 1st March at 13.30.

Under the provisions of Clause 27 of the Appeals Procedure, you are hereby instructed to provide your teachers Jay, Kay and Ell, with the documents relating to this case immediately.

The documents are this letter, together with

1.   page 61 of the Ministry of Education Decision Paper

2.   the "Zed Incident" report by Assistant Inspector Dee

3.   page 14 of the "Appeals - Ministry of Education" document

4.   your letter asking for an Appeal.

Please point out to the three teachers that the "Zed Incident" report is private and confidential, and must not be revealed to anyone who is not connected with the hearing of the Appeal.

R. Ess.

Appeals Administrator

MINISTRY OF EDUCATION
                                          Ministry House
                                          Linguan City

The "Zed Incident"

To whom it may concern:

I was requested by both the Inspectorate and the Head Teacher of Blue
School to investigate the so-called "Zed Incident". My report is
based on an interview with Mrs Zed in hospital, and with 10 students
(chosen at random), who were in Mrs Zed's class at the time the
incident took place. Although witnesses differed in respect of some
details of the incident, there was general agreement that what
happened was as follows:

Mrs Zed told the class of about 35 students (in their 3rd year of
learning English) that she had invented a simulation which would give
them practice and confidence in using English. She described it as
"a game called 'Walking the Tightrope'". Mrs Zed explained to the
class that in a simulation the students are responsible for their own
behaviour; they had a job to do; and she said the teacher (herself)
would not interfere. (One or two of the students said they were
amazed and delighted to hear this.)

Mrs Zed then drew a chalk line down the centre of the room to
represent the tightrope. The class was divided into two groups,
called the Red Group and the Blue Group, one at each side of the
"tightrope".

In order to play the game, one person from each group had to take it
in turn to "walk the tightrope" - that is, walk down the chalk line
as if it were a tightrope in a circus. The group to which the
tightrope walker belonged had to say words of encouragement. Mrs Zed
said she gave as examples - "Well done", "Good work" and "Keep it up"
The opposing group, on the other hand, were expected to utter words
of discouragement, like "It is dangerous", "You might fall" and "Go
back".

Mrs Zed then stood at the back of the room and watched what happened.
The result was a rapid escalation into violence and absurdity. Talk
became shouting, shouts became insults, insults became threats, and
threats became physical attack. At this point Mrs Zed intervened with
only partial success to try to separate the two groups, who were
fighting each other.

The noise brought the Head Teacher to the scene and order was
restored. Mrs Zed was taken home in a shocked condition, and the
next day went to hospital where she is under observation.

The class was taken over by Teacher Jay. There were no further
attempts at simulations, and behaviour has been excellent.

                                   Assistant Inspector Dee
                                              17th January

Teacher Ell

Like my colleagues, I have had no personal experience of simulations. This is a point of danger in our Appeal. If we are not
careful, the inspectors will say, 'All you need is a bit of practice in
simulations and then you can start using the technique.' They will
then report that the whole problem can be solved with a bit of
teacher training.

Even if we were simulation experts, it would not solve our
problems. Our main problem is that the general ability of our
students is lower and their home background is much worse than
in most schools. This means that if we are to do our duty as
teachers, we cannot afford to waste time on non-essentials. A
good examination result is tremendously important to these
students' futures. It makes sense that we should concentrate our
teaching efforts on the essentials.

The Zed incident damaged the school in the eyes of the parents.
What damages a school also damages the Ministry, and might
even damage the Government.

knew the experiment could be a flop, but I preferred experiment to expectation. I preferred to take the chance that it
would not work, and to find out why, rather than to make
guesses.

In the event, I needn't have worried. The discussion at the
Ministry went on for forty-five minutes and could have gone on
longer had the time not run out. The extract shows, I think, the
considerable degree of sophisticated thought (as distinct from
sophisticated language) used by these children on the subject of
simulations in relation to the philosophy, psychology and
methodology of education:

Kay We did this Tightrope thing, which was not an academic
type simulation. It got out of hand. We can't do simulations
properly because we have large classes. If we had smaller
classes or more teachers we might be able to do it. They were
just treating it as a game.

Bee Do you think it is a good idea, when you are teaching
your pupils, that you don't do a stroke, you just sit them

down with their worksheets and their paper? If you give them simulations, then they can do what they want to, can't they?

Kay They definitely did not want to do it.

Ai But isn't that put down to the fact that the teacher wasn't controlling the class properly, and couldn't control the class?

Ell You shouldn't have to control people if the lessons were any good. What happened was that they just started fighting.

Cee Yes, but don't you think that when kids learn a new thing they always sort of treat it as a joke at first, don't they, before they get used to it? So don't you think that was the initial thing of it?

Kay What do you think then, of simulations?

Cee I think, personally, that simulations are a good idea because . . .

Kay Because it's cheap?

Cee No, not because it's cheap, because it's, it's . . . if you are always telling children what to do, then when they leave school that teacher sort of thing isn't there. There isn't teachers outside telling them what to do, so they've got to be able to do things for themselves. And if you do simulations then you are giving them practice in this activity.

Jay Simulations should have been introduced earlier in the school. You can teach the basics of simulations in the infant school, and then develop it in the secondary school.

Ai Isn't infant school a bit too young? They are just breaking in to school then. They've just come from the home. They wouldn't really understand it, would they?

Jay Why not? You could introduce it in a simple sense . . .

A few minutes after the end of the simulation, one of the boys (Inspector Bee) came to me and said, 'I've just realized, we were talking about ourselves'. The thought had just struck him. He had been so involved at the Ministry of Education in Lingua City that he had not realized that the hearing had been about 14-year-olds in schools in the East End of London.

One particularly interesting aspect of this transcript is that the children in the role of the teachers argued in favour of introducing simulations at an early age, whereas when I had tried out the simulation with various groups of teachers, those in the roles of Jay, Kay and Ell had all argued that simulations should be introduced later, not earlier. This seems to support my general experience that in the case of simulations most teachers have expectations which are lower than the subsequent achievements of the participants. It is very common to find that teachers are surprised and pleased at the way their children tackle simulations.

These particular children later created a simulation of their own in which they devised roles for a group of eight people – elderly judge, prostitute, famous footballer, bank robber, etc. – and the problem was to decide which six should be allowed into the nuclear fallout shelter. They then participated in their own simulation.

The above examples show that it is not too difficult to involve pupils or students in creating their own simulations, particularly if they have already participated in simulations.

Whether you decide to ask your class to create simulations is a question depending very much on circumstances, including your own experience of using, choosing and creating simulations.

It is an option worth considering, particularly as you can put your toe in the water before deciding whether to dive in. You can find out easily and quickly whether your pupils/students can design simulations by asking them 'What might happen next?' at the conclusion of a simulation. Or, in the course of normal teaching, you can take an idea or event as a starting-point for exploring the simulation potential, and ask the four key questions.

Once you have seen how they respond to this challenge, you can decide whether or not to allow the class to swim in this particular pool.

· 3 · Writing the documents

Types of documents

By 'documents' I mean anything that is included in the answer to the question 'What do they do it with?' In the case of the two teachers devising a simulation about Crusader castle-building, the answer was 'sand'. There are simulations where the answer would be a computer, a computer program, a piece of film or building blocks. But in almost all cases the author of a simulation has to write something. Usually these are role cards, background information in scenario form or incorporated into facsimile documents, and possibility artifacts which represent things (money, prestige, spears, houses, heart attacks).

In addition to these documents for the participants there are the organizer's notes (controller's notes, teacher's manual). These are the explanations and instructions about how to run the simulation, and they usually include a description of the aims, plus hints about following up the event in the debriefing afterwards. Compared with writing the documents for the action, which can be quite exciting, the writing of the organizer's notes may seem rather tedious. So you don't have to write the notes if you restrict your simulations to your own class. On the other hand, as mentioned in chapter 6, there are definite intellectual advantages in writing the notes, not least because the discipline helps you to sort things out in your own mind.

I write 'notes for participants' for all my simulations. Few other authors have adopted this idea, but I find it helpful to explain directly to the participants what the simulation is all about, and what they can do and cannot do. Normally, the notes would be handed out at the briefing, or perhaps in the planning stages. Sometimes the teacher and students go through the document together, and discuss the mechanics of the event.

These notes might include some reference to the simulation technique, and how it differs from other methods. I write various warnings about not treating it as a game, not play-acting, and not inventing 'facts' to win arguments, depending on the nature of the individual simulation. For example, 'Survival' contains map squares which are handed out by the organizer as requested by the participants according to which direction they decide to take. Since this might seem like a game, I stress that this is not the case.

Strictly speaking, the notes for participants should not be necessary, since they do no more than repeat points which could be made by the organizer. But experience of having the job of organizer has taught me how easy it is to forget a key point, and then be forced to interrupt the action to say, 'Sorry, I should have told you before you started that you must not . . . .' This mentally jerks the participants out of their roles and back to being students, and then another jerk into their roles again. Another advantage of using notes for participants is that they can include the list of the documents, thus guarding against the organizer forgetting to hand something out before the action begins.

If you include a reference to the nature of the simulation technique in the notes, this helps to safeguard the simulation against accidental sabotage if it is run by other teachers.

NOTES FOR PARTICIPANTS *SURVIVAL*

What it's about

In both *Red Desert* and *Shipwrecked* you are survivors and it is your job to stay alive.

The five profiles in *Red Desert* and in *Shipwrecked* explain the situation. Read them carefully, they are important.

You start with one map square. When you have decided which way to travel, the organizer will give you another map square. You have a diary to record your day-to-day movements from square to square.

There are no diagonal moves, and you all stick together.

The organizer will brief you on the 'rules'. But don't ask the organizer for advice on which way to go. There is no teacher with you in the hostile environment. You are alone. You are in charge. Your survival depends on you alone.

Advice

Decide on how you are going to determine which way to go – will you have a leader who decides, will you vote, or will you just hope for the best?

SURVIVAL may look like a game of chance, but it is not. If you treat it like a game then you are not likely to survive. Try to think yourself into the situation, try to see yourself in the hostile environment.

Put a small coin or marker on the square you are on, and move it when you move. It helps to see yourself in the situation, and it helps the person with the diary to fill it in correctly.

In *Shipwrecked* remember to ask for the cards marked 'spears', 'ropes' and 'raft' when you are entitled to them. If you forget to ask for the cards at the proper time then you will not have the spears, ropes and raft when you need them.

Non-sequential authorship

The documents (including equipment) can all be introduced at the beginning of the simulation, or sequentially as the event progresses. But the actual writing of these documents does not have to be in any particular sequence. Not only can you write the documents without a design blueprint, it is possible to be writing a document for some non-simulation purpose – writing a memo or private letter – and you might suddenly get the idea, 'This might work well in a simulation', and you can take it on from there.

If you are fascinated by any particular document, or artifact, then tackle it, write it up and see if the simulation can be built around it. If, for example, you telephone someone and hear the recorded voice from a telephone-answering machine then it might occur to you to wonder if it could be used in a simulation. Could the 'document' be a tape of people telephoning, the participant(s) being required to take action as a result of the messages? The messages could be about business or murder or sex or politics or seat belts. I don't know of such a simulation, but it's an idea if you want to use it.

Whatever documents (artifacts, etc.) that you produce, there are certain commonsense principles which you should think about from time to time during authorship.

Reality of function

The documents should assist reality of function. If they don't then you should ask yourself whether you are really trying to design a simulation or whether you are inventing a case study or an informal drama or a game or a teacher-controlled exercise or an accumulation of facts which require learning. A role card which begins 'You are angry . . .' is suitable for an informal drama or a bit of role play, but it is inconsistent with reality of function. A simulation is not superior to any other techniques, it is just different. So it is important that you should consider whether a simulation is the best means of achieving what you have in mind.

Simulated and structured environment

Enough materials should be provided for sustaining reality of function, but there should not be so much that the participants have great difficulty in sorting out which bits are useful, unless, of course, one of your aims is to give them practice in dealing with a mass of documentation. The documents should be consistent with each other, and it should be reasonably clear which is a 'fact' and which is an 'opinion'.

The mechanics of the simulation

The procedures should enable the simulation to proceed smoothly, without the participants having to ask 'What are we supposed to do now?' If the mechanics of the event entail part-time roles, what happens to these students when they are not participants? Is it absolutely necessary to have part-time roles? If two groups each have different tasks, what happens if one group finishes long before the other group?

Another question of mechanics occurs when the documents pose a choice between solution A and solution B. Are the participants allowed to look around for other options?

If the simulation involves a committee or a parliament, what are the general rules of procedure? Has the president of the Assembly full powers to adjourn a meeting at any point, or must the discussion continue until the school bell rings? If there is a situation where a vote may occur, does the person in the chair have the casting vote?

If the role cards contain opinions, can the participants change their views, or must they always repeat the opinions given on their cards? If the participants ask, 'What happens if we can't agree?' does the organizer have to answer this question?

There are plenty of ways of dealing with these issues, as will be seen later in this book, the main one being the recommendation that the participants should be entitled to behave in whatever way seems appropriate in the circumstances, and with whatever powers, duties and responsibilities they would normally have in such a position. But the point is that you should, from time to time, ask yourself some awkward questions about the mechanics of your simulation. Don't assume that everything will be rosy.

These three categories involving some general principles of simulation design – function, environment and mechanics – are not watertight compartments. Successful authorship requires flexibility, and it does not help to allocate role cards to the first category, the scenario to the second and the notes for participants to the third. The three groups of principles should be allowed freedom to mix.

Fact or fiction?

An important decision is whether the simulated background should be fact or fiction. Most teachers would probably choose the option of making it factual without giving the matter much thought, since this fits in with the educational aim of making lessons relevant. There is a strong temptation to use not only factual material but local fact. Teachers who go down this road would, wherever plausible (and perhaps when implausible), tailor the roles to fit the age, sex, nationality, race, religion, abilities and interests of the participants, and build the public documents on real and local geographical features, institutions, buildings, schools, businesses, media, environmental issues, and so on.

However, simulations are not the same as projects and case studies. Different considerations apply. There are dangers lurking along the path of localization. The most obvious is that if you set your mind firmly on the need for providing local fact then you will not write a simulation at all, but a project or an exercise. To concentrate on modelling local reality may seriously limit the decision-making opportunities of the participants for several reasons:

1 There may be too many facts in the documents and role cards.
2 Many facts may be irrelevant to the action.

3 Several roles can be extremely factual, but extremely part-time or extremely boring.
4 The arguments can be one-sided.
5 The simulation may keep grinding to a halt by disputes about what is, and what is not, a local fact.
6 The participants may think that what matters is to reproduce what happened in the real event, or what usually happens, and assume that this is the right answer.

This final point is fairly crucial. It focuses attention on whether the activity is supposed to be a simulation or a piece of role-play in which the correct behaviour is to mimic some particular event.

As far as authorship is concerned, the main danger is that whenever you are faced with a choice between what is fact and what is interesting (provocative, humorous, imaginative), there will be a strong temptation to choose the factual, to the detriment of the simulation as an event.

There are several positive virtues in using fiction rather than fact. It is much easier to manipulate fiction than fact. There is more flexibility. The power of an author to add, alter or remove conventions, institutions, geographical features and so on is extremely valuable. It enables the author to concentrate on the essential issues, including the smooth running of the simulation.

Using a fictitious background also has the merits of allowing all the participants to start from scratch. This can benefit the less academic students who usually start an activity several steps behind those students who are better informed of the facts of a particular situation.

In addition, fiction gives a simulation a universality which not only helps authorship and the smooth running of the event, but may assist in the debriefing. Being fictional may, paradoxically, make the simulation more relevant to the participants since they can contrast it with what they know and thus appreciate more clearly the distinctiveness or otherwise of their locality.

Other considerations arise if you are thinking of trying to get your simulations published. A fictional simulation may have a wider market because of its universality. The inclusion of factual documents may cause copyright problems, and the insertion of provocative material into a factual simulation might libel someone. A factual simulation can get out of date, and a number of published simulations have to be updated every few years to take into account changes in law, prices, supplementary benefits, political parties or international politics. Facts change, fiction does not. An interesting case is the change in the title of a simulation published in 1975 by Community Service Volunteers entitled 'Greenham Gypsy Site'. The name Greenham was changed in 1984 because of its connection with women protesting against Cruise missiles at Greenham Common. It is now 'Greenwood Gypsy Site'.

My argument is not that you should avoid writing a simulation using local facts, but that you should not do so as an automatic reflex in the name of 'relevancy'. I hope the considerations listed above will help clarify the issue of whether you should use facts or fiction. And since many other decisions about authorship will follow from this one, it is a good idea to take it early and get it right.

Role cards and facts

The most frequent mistake when writing role cards is the failure to give a clear answer to the four key questions – What is the problem? Who are the participants? What do they have to do? What do they have to do it with?

Let's begin by looking at some of the role cards in a simulation on a familiar theme – local reactions to a building project – 'Spring Green Motorway'. This was written by Community Service Volunteers plus Stephen Joseph and Nick Lester, and is one of several simulations published by CSV and related to local issues.

Ms June Finlay
You are a young, talented reporter on the Ildridge Gazette. You used to work in London, but gave up possible promotion there to move to the country which you love. You know that the Department of Transport have offered to pay Lord Smirk £100,000 for this land and intend to raise the point at the public meeting.

Generally speaking, when you are are writing a role card it is best to avoid any personality characteristics unless they are essential to the action. If you state the sex, a participant of the opposite sex might be tempted to mimic masculine or feminine behaviour. If you state age, participants of a different age might start imitating age characteristics. If you state that a person is good at their job, this might intimidate since the participants might feel they are expected to reach a professional standard rather than the purely functional 'Do the best you can in the situation in which you find yourself.'

The card for Ms June Finlay commits all these faults. She is female, she is young, and she is talented in her job. In addition, the role card is vague about what is true and what is an allegation. This is particularly important when allegations about impropriety or corruption are being made.

Finlay's role card contains conclusions but few facts on which the conclusions are based. So if asked, 'Why do you believe this?', no sensible answer is available.

Finlay could reply:

1 'Because that's what it says on my role card,' but that is to step outside the simulation; or
2 'I don't know,' which sounds inadequate and stupid; or
3 'I will not tell you,' which sounds churlish; or
4 'Because X, Y and Z,' in which case the participant has taken on the role of author, inventor or magician.

Since no one wants to be humiliated in public, it is worth noting some of the dangers involved if Finlay chose to invent 'facts' in order to help the simulation along. At the public meeting Finlay could be faced with some very awkward questions. For example:

> You say you know that the Department of Transport have offered to pay Lord Smirk £100,000 for the land – who told you that? Do you claim that the money is more than the land is worth? You refer to possible corruption – do you intend to print this allegation in your newspaper? Are you aware that there is a law of libel?
>
> If you are a talented reporter, as you claim, why do you ask questions at a public meeting – or are you confusing this meeting with a news conference? I take your point that you love the country, but is it not true that you are so biased against the motorway that you will twist any fact in order to discredit the people involved?

When you are designing a simulation it is very important that you should decide what the key 'facts' are, and make sure that they are available to the participants who might need to refer to them in their role cards, or else incorporate the facts in the other documents.

In the above example, Finlay should know where the information came from about the £100,000 allegation, and whether this is supposed to be a scandal. Presumably the sum is supposed to be too high, otherwise why is it mentioned at all? There is no information about how much the land is worth. The other role cards for the three people who might know this, Lord Smirk and two Ministry officials (see pp. 44–5), are unhelpful, except that Lord Smirk's card says he has been offered £100,000. There is nothing to suggest any dishonesty, bribery, corruption or improper conduct.

It can be seen that Williams and Benson also have problems concerning 'What do they have to do?' If both are supposed to function professionally and impartially, why is Williams told that one of the reasons he favours the motorway is that without the project he might have no work to do, and why is Benson told that she personally opposes the project if she is not supposed to show this in some way or other? If they address the meeting before Lord Smirk what do they say if asked by Ms Finlay about the £100,000? They might deny the allegation, and where would that leave Lord Smirk?

Role Card   MR ERNEST WILLIAMS

You come from the section of the Department of Transport responsible for designing and building the road. You think the road is needed because it is an important section of the national network and also because you might have no work to do in the office if the scheme does not go ahead. You're sorry that a few people in the village will suffer from the motorway but think that the benefits to the country outweigh any disadvantages to people in Spring Green.

Role Card   MRS ANN BENSON

You are a Senior Official in the Department of the Environment. You have been asked by the Minister to report on the outcome of the meeting. You have come to Spring Green by train as you have never driven a car. Although you have a Departmental Chauffeur, you prefer travelling by train. As a civil servant you must of course be unbiased, but personally you support environmental protection.

Role Card   LORD SMIRK

Your ancestors have lived in Spring Green since the Middle Ages – Baron Smirk (1372) was the original Lord of the Manor of Spring Green. You like the country life and you occasionally take your seat in the House of Lords, having inherited your title and Smirk Manor only two years ago. You like rabbit shooting, horse riding and fast cars. Dunton Farm is one of the farms on your enormous estate, which covers 2,000 acres. The Department have offered you £100,000 for the land on your estate which they want to purchase for the motorway.

Lord Smirk seems to be invited to play-act the role of a selfish, self-satisfied aristocrat. Both his name and his portrait (p. 46) suggest this, as does the information that he 'occasionally' takes his seat in the House of Lords. His activities are those of personal pleasure, and there is no mention of managing the estate. So instead of behaving functionally in the role, he might play it for laughs.

It is in simulations where the role cards are intended for individuals rather than groups that particular care should be taken by the author in order to avoid leaving individuals vulnerable to attack. Plenty of examples exist in published simulations in which an individual role is deliberately or inadvertently marked down for attack, as will be seen later when considering the role of the landlord in 'Tenement'.

Some participants, of course, can enjoy play-acting the villain, but others may not be so extrovert. In any case, it is bad simulation design to introduce stereotypes. Usually there is no good reason to produce role cards implying that landlords are greedy, landowners are selfish, politicians are corrupt or, for that matter, workers are idle.

LORD SMIRK

Stereotype roles are bad not only because they may leave participants open to attack, but because they strip that person of some of the power which is an essential ingredient in a simulation. If one or two participants refuse to discuss questions rationally because of vices implanted in their personalities by the role cards, others may follow suit, and either play-act or stubbornly refuse to consider any opinion other than their own.

Public or private documents?

Having sorted out which are the key facts, it is best to embody them in one of the public documents which can be read by all, or else write them into at least two of the individual documents. This is to safeguard against someone not reading their role cards properly, or claiming that the role card contains information which it does not contain. It is easy to duplicate the key facts, and the possible consequences of not doing so can be harmful to the smooth running of the simulation.

If, however, an important fact is unlikely to be known by any of the participants, it can be left out. As in the real world, decisions may have to be made without a full knowledge of all the relevant information. Doubts and ambiguities are perfectly acceptable in a simulation, but they should not be so extensive that the participants say, 'I know we've only just sat down at this meeting, but as so many key facts are missing we may as well adjourn until the position is clarified.'

A frequent mistake made by authors of conflict-type simulations is to have no public documents, but to divide the facts into two, and to give each group only those facts which support their own case.

One simulation designed by staff at a teacher-training college dealt with wage negotiations at a local (fictitious) company. The two sides had their own private documents containing information about the situation. A key fact was obviously the going rate for the job in that area. The private document for the trade-union side said that a local firm making a similar product had just awarded a pay rise of 17 per cent. The private document for the employer's side said that one local firm had reached agreement with its workers that there should be a nil pay rise that year because of the general level of unemployment and financial problems.

The participants on both sides would probably assume that the information they had been given was not highly selective since it would be extremely stupid for negotiators to come to the table knowing only half the story. They would wish to know the full facts, and in the case of local wage negotiations it would be very easy for both sides to find out the average rate of pay rises. In negotiations, of course, each side could select examples favourable to their own case, but they would not be speaking from ignorance when they did so.

It is not difficult to imagine the problem facing the participants when the two sides met. 'The going rate is 17 per cent for this sort of job.' 'No, it isn't, it is a nil rate because of the unemployment and financial difficulties.' 'No, it isn't.' 'Yes, it is.' 'Excuse me, sir, our bit of paper says it is 17 per cent for one firm, and their bit of paper says there was no pay rise in another firm. We want to know the average pay rise for local firms.' Once participants start referring to 'our bit of paper' rather than 'the report produced by our Finance Department', their respect for the author is diminishing.

The conclusion to be drawn from these examples is that a smooth-running simulation:

1 must contain the important facts, which
2 must be available (in public or private documents or both) to all who would normally have access to them.

Muddle about key facts produces conflict, but it is conflict between the participants and the author (or the organizer). It is difficult to see why so many simulations fail to supply the key facts, or else muddle the issue. After all, the main facts are the essential data of a simulation. It might be that some authors are not clear about the concept of a simulation, or a simulation might have been designed by a committee which did not co-ordinate well. Perhaps an author did not see eye to eye with a client. Possibly some aspects of the simulation were rewritten, and the implications of these changes in other areas were overlooked. If, while writing the details, you bear in mind your answers to the four key questions mentioned in the last chapter (Problem? Who? Do what? With what?), it is not difficult to harmonize the parts with the whole.

Educational objectives

Educational objectives can help or hinder simulation design. By educational objectives I mean concepts which embrace educational values, not simply the label of a subject area. 'I want to design a business simulation' is merely a statement of area, but 'I want to write a good interactive business simulation' includes values. So if the author bears in mind 'good' and 'interactive' this may help in tackling some problems of design, such as whether the participants should work on their own or in groups. It follows from this that any worthwhile objective cannot be left behind at the first step, as suggested by some academic authors, but must be a guiding principle throughout the design process.

If the educational objectives are implicit in the simulation technique itself – to enhance participant power, to produce sufficient facts to sustain reality of function – the objectives help the design, but are somewhat self-evident since they add up to no more than saying that the author is trying to write a simulation which works well. But if the objectives are external to the technique, these may or may not be a handicap to designing a good workable interesting simulation.

Consider four external objectives: (1) the teaching of a message, (2) the learning of facts, (3) the assessment of learning, and (4) the arousal of feelings.

Message simulations

Many simulations begin life as a message. They owe their origins to a desire by their authors to convey some concept of educational value. This occurs when people design simulations in order to place their organization or ideas in a good light. The message could be moral, political, economic, humanitarian or just plain 'Our firm is best.' As a result, there is a tendency to try to bias the event in favour of the message, giving strong arguments to the proponents of the message, and weak, or even disreputable, arguments to those who oppose it.

My objection to this is not that there is anything disreputable about using a simulation to put over a message, but that it often results in a mish-mash activity, an uneasy mixture of genuine simulation with play-acting, caricature and stereotypes.

We have already seen some degree of bias in 'Spring Green Motorway', where the roles of Finlay, Benson and Williams should have been neutral. In 'Tenement', produced by the charity organization Shelter, there are roles for six individuals or families in a dilapidated property, for welfare and state agencies, and one role for the landlord. Unlike the tenants, the landlord is given no name. The landlord has a sex (male) and the role card contains his picture, which verges on caricature.

THE LANDLORD

The description on the landlord's card gives him a personality – a mixture of greed, stupidity and lack of conscience:

> The house is not in good condition. . . . You are not particularly concerned about the conditions. There is a housing shortage in the town and you know there will always be people willing to rent the rooms. . . . They [the Campbell family] are West Indian and you charge them an excessive rent because you know they will find it difficult to find accommodation elsewhere. . . . This woman [Emily Brown] has been left by the man living with her whom you suspect was not her husband. Because the child is young she is not able to work and you are wondering how she will pay the rent now that the man has left. You are considering finding some excuse to evict her. . . . This family [the Johnston family] owe you £72 in rent. You have given them notice to quit and if they are not out by tomorrow you intend to evict them by force.

This role seems an open invitation to melodrama rather than finding some sort of rationale for behaviour. After all, why seek an excuse to evict Emily Brown before she starts to default on the rent? She might find a way of continuing to pay the money. So the landlord is not only supposed to be greedy and unfeeling, but stupid as well, not to mention ignorant of the law regarding landlord and tenant.

The role card of the Johnston family says, 'the landlord has said he will forcibly evict you.' Consequently, forcible eviction is a key issue in 'Tenement'. But the only reference to anything illegal is at the end of the role card for the Voluntary Housing Aid Centre: 'A landlord cannot evict a tenant without a Possession Order from the County Court.' There is no mention of the fact that under the Rent Act 1965 it is not only illegal, it is a criminal offence for anyone to try to evict a tenant without a court order or to try to make the tenant leave by using force, by threatening the tenant or the tenant's family, or by interfering with the tenant's home or possessions.

The role card for the Local Authority Housing Department, which should have included something about forcible eviction, does not mention it, and refers only to how it might help a family after it has been evicted. Nor is illegal eviction mentioned in the cards for the Local Authority Environmental Health Department, the Rent Office or the Citizens' Advice Bureau.

So if none of the tenants visit the Voluntary Housing Aid Centre they will not learn that eviction without a court order is illegal, let alone that the use of force or the threat of force is a criminal offence. This omission may stir up the emotional temperature of the event, and even endanger the safety of the landlord. The tenants are likely to protest against the 'system'. This may be part of the message, but it hardly serves the pursuit of truth.

Another example of a simulation with a message is 'North Sea Challenge' produced by BP Educational Service. This consists of three simulations about a fictitious oil company, Norsoco. In each simulation the point is made that Norsoco is extremely concerned about preserving the environment.

In the first simulation, 'Strike', we learn from a news item that a Norsoco spokesman has said, 'If a pipeline were to be laid, every effort would be made to interfere as little as possible with the environment.'

In the second simulation, 'Slick', there is a letter addressed to the Local Pollution Officer at a Scottish port about the need for contingency plans to deal with a possible oil slick. This letter does not come from the Department for the Environment, or from the Ministry of Agriculture and Fisheries, it comes from Norsoco's Environment Control Manager.

The third simulation, 'Impact', is about a Norsoco plan to build a site for constructing steel platforms for oil-drilling at Stomar or Inverlochen – two fictitious Scottish ports. All the role cards for those in favour of the Norsoco plan consist of rational arguments – more jobs, a development of the area, etc. But those against are not always so rational.

J. Morton

If God had wanted us to have North Sea oil he wouldn't have put it at the bottom of the North Sea. That's your opinion and you are very angry about the proposed development. Your husband was buried in the cemetery near the proposed site and you believe it's a sacrilege that English oil companies should be exploiting Scottish oil and trampling all over the countryside ruining the local amenities. They'll all be gone when they've got all their money anyway.

Morton's card is likely to be regarded as an invitation to play-act a religious crank, who believes that God did not intend man to drill for oil anywhere. As in the case of the landlord in 'Tenement' this role pushes the event in favour of the message by discrediting the opposition. It is incompatible with the simulation technique because it encourages play-acting, not only of the caricature of one role, but of the feeling of acting out an event so that it reaches a predetermined result.

I have always felt that simulations are unsuitable for messages since the participants become sensitive to any attempt to manipulate them down a chosen path to the 'right' answer. And even if they go down this path during the action, perhaps because they want the simulation to succeed as an event, they can take their revenge in the debriefing when they point out that 'it is not like that in real life.'

It is more difficult to get away with distorted or omitted facts in a simulation because simulations usually involve groups rather than isolated individuals. It is necessary for only one or two of the participants (or the organizer) to know the true facts and tell the others. Messages are more likely to be accepted when there is a one-way flow of information from the author to the passive reader, viewer or listener.

However, not all organizations which produce simulations build in a bias in favour of a message, nor is it the case that all organizations which sponsor simulations do so only if the simulations are connected with their own business. Coca-Cola Export Corporation published a simulation, 'Man in His Environment', which had nothing to do with soft drinks but was concerned with a series of development projects in a particular locality. The British Oxygen Company sponsored a series of simulations under the title 'Five Simple Business Games', which had nothing to do with the production or marketing of oxygen, but had such titles as 'Gorgeous Gateaux Ltd' and 'Dart Aviation Ltd'. In this latter simulation the participants actually build paper-dart aeroplanes which have to fly (glide) to certain specifications.

Fact-teaching simulations

The fact-teaching motive also tends towards creating an event which is not a simulation. The temptation is to load the simulation with facts, making it difficult to run, and introducing a 'Learn the facts' motive, which is the motive of a student, rather than 'Do the best you can in the situation in which you find yourselves' motive, which is the motive of a participant in a simulation.

Ten or twenty years ago it was not uncommon to find that the simulation had no role cards, no facsimile documents, but only a scenario document – and usually a pretty massive one at that – which had to be read by all participants before the action began. This could take hours, days or even weeks. The author, striving to convey the facts of history, business, geography and so on, had shoved in great wodges of material taken directly from the textbooks on the subject. Even today it is not all that unusual to find huge chunks of facts and figures which have no conceivable relevance to the likely course of the action. But in general today's authors are more aware of the value of simulations as a practice ground for communication skills, social skills, organizational skills and language skills.

If the reason for the fact-teaching objective is to help students pass those sort of examinations which are dominated by remembrance of facts, then the results could be unfortunate. The students may learn only those facts which help the action from their particular roles, and produce an unbalanced answer in the examinations. Another danger is that the historical facts may become confused with the facts created during the action. A simulation on the Roundheads and Cavaliers can be so motivating that the students may confuse the Civil War with their own campaigns and diplomacy, causing the examiners to wonder where the students got their answers from. If the object is to teach facts, more appropriate methods are available – textbooks, projects and case studies.

You may feel that if simulations are not particularly good at conveying facts, that diminishes their value. But facts can be learned after a simulation as well as during the event. An imaginative simulation which is not laden with facts often encourages the participants to go to the library. They might say, 'That simulation on trade union rights was a good experience, so let's find out whether we could have appealed on that point John brought up.' Also, because a good simulation is a memorable event, it can serve as an efficient peg for learning and recalling what the students discover in the library (or in a television programme, newspaper, etc.). Simulations can produce long-term motivation for learning, as distinct from short-term neat answers. Consequently, the participants may learn more facts as a result of a simulation which has few facts than they do from a simulation which is loaded with facts.

Assessment simulations

If the objective is to assess previous learning, this may have a favourable or an unfavourable effect on the design. It will be favourable if the natural course of the action brings out whether participants have understood the previous learning. But it will be unfavourable if the action itself is punctuated with assessment points which are external to the nature of the event.

The last chapter contained an imaginary example of teachers devising a castle-building simulation to round off a project on Crusader castles, and the point was made that, whether they intended it or not, the simulation would also have the effect of assessing how much the pupils had understood. It would, of course, have been easy to produce a traditional type of examination paper where each child had to answer questions about castles. But it is one thing to be able to remember details of castles, and quite another to be able to understand them sufficiently well to be able to use the facts.

The first institutionalized use of simulations for assessment is usually attributed to the Prussian Army in the later nineteenth century. They were introduced for the purpose of assessing the quality of candidates for officer training. A series of simulations were devised to test the skills and qualities required, and this replaced the former method of relying entirely on interviews and pencil-and-paper tests. The British Army then became a leading pioneer in devising simulations to assess, and also to train, soldiers, and this spread during the Second World War to the United States for the selection of agents and spies. This led to simulations being used widely in business, a technique which grew fairly rapidly and is now world-wide, often being conducted at so-called Assessment Centres (sometimes courses rather than centres). It was argued that there is no difference in principle between simulations to assess spies or managers, or any other job for that matter. The procedure is to decide what are the main characteristics required in the behaviour, and then to devise simulations (or case studies or improvisation exercises) which can be used to assess these qualities.

The normal method of assessment is to observe the behaviour. But in education there is a temptation to bypass such assessment by building in a point-scoring mechanism, and the question arises whether this is appropriate, and whether there are any disadvantages in so doing.

In business simulations, which are now fairly common in education and in business, it is not unusual to measure success by the amount of profit of the group running the business. A group running the country's economy is deemed successful if it achieves a satisfactory balance of payments, rate of inflation, etc. These are normal measures of achievement in the real world. Therefore, from the point of view of the mechanics and smooth running of the simulation there is nothing to object to in such scoring mechanisms. Whether the achievement reflected by such scores was due to skill or luck is another matter entirely.

But if, for example, 'welfare points' or 'environment preservation marks' are added into the totals for profit and loss, the activity has changed character. It has lost some degree of plausibility and reality of function. From a simulation it has been moved to something much nearer a game. What is likely to happen is not that the participants will be concerned about welfare and the environment, but that they will try to achieve the maximum number of points. And if, in any of the examples of simulations already discussed, the participants were awarded marks within the activity for successfully doing this or that, or had marks deducted for failure to behave in a particular way, it is extremely doubtful whether the activity could be classified as a simulation.

The question to ask yourself when creating your simulations is whether you need marks, points, scores, and if you do, are they plausible? If they are not plausible, would it not be better to design a genuine game where the motive is to score points and win?

Simulations which arouse feelings

A complete contrast to devising a point-scoring mechanism is the desire to introduce feelings into a simulation. It is difficult to put it more precisely. What I'm referring to are emotions, personal attitudes, sympathy and a deeper understanding than is possible with a purely rational assessment of the situation.

Feelings have important educational implications. Events

and concepts are often more memorable when associated with feelings, yet feelings tend to be ignored in the classroom in favour of fact-learning. Feelings can aid fact-learning, and serve as a peg in the search for knowledge. In addition, feelings are intimately connected with humanity, with human rights and dignity. This relates to attitudes of self-respect and respect for others, which for many people are vital benefits of the simulation technique.

Feelings can be aroused in a simulation because of the subject matter, as was seen in the case of 'Tenement' where considerable sympathy and anger emerge. But in this section I wish to refer particularly to certain devices which can arouse feelings, rather than simply the subject matter itself.

Several American authors are outstanding at introducing devices which evoke (or provoke) feelings in simulations. Cathy Greenblat, a professor of sociology at Rutgers University and editor of the journal *Simulation and Games*, designed a simulation in collaboration with John Gagnon about haemophilia. This disease is not just a matter of a person bleeding a lot when they cut a finger. The serious attacks are often internal bleeding. The aim of the Greenblat/Gagnon simulation is not to show people what it is like to be a haemophiliac, which is impossible, but to give an insight into the problems of the disease, including the health-care aspects, and the sort of feelings that can be associated with the problems.

If, for example, a haemophiliac is suffering from a severe attack of internal bleeding, it is not a good thing to wait in a queue at a doctor's surgery, nor to be impeded by bureaucratic delays, nor (if there is no national health service) to be handicapped by lack of money to pay for the treatment. In the United States a haemophiliac might at any time be in a situation requiring medical treatment, blood and the financial resources to pay for them.

At this point you might like to go and make a cup of tea and try to work out how this event could be designed as (1) a game, (2) a routine simulation, and (3) a simulation involving feelings and emotions. You might also like to think of a good title for it.

As mentioned earlier in relation to 'Talking Rocks', this is the sort of exercise you could consider giving to your students to help clarify concepts and stretch imaginations.

By the time your eye reaches this paragraph you may have designed the outline of a game, plus a couple of simulations; you can compare your own results with the following options.

As a game there are plenty of ways of dealing with the situation of haemophilia and health care. An obvious one is to make it a board game with dice, chance cards, money and counters. Some squares on the board could be coloured yellow to represent mild attacks, and red squares indicate severe attacks. Chance cards could decide (1) the speed of the treatment, and (2) the benefits of proper after-care. Money could be collected as a wage each time round the board, and/or it could be the subject of the chance cards or particular squares on the board. There could be two piles of chance cards, one for people who land on yellow squares and the other for those who land on red squares. If a person had received suitable medical treatment, then this could be in the form of a token allowing them to transfer to a yellow square the next time they landed on a red square or freeing them from any penalty if they landed on a yellow square.

After playing such a game the players would be aware of the need for rapid treatment and good after-care and also of the need for people to understand the problems of haemophiliacs. What the game does not do is give the players any power. They are at the mercy of chance. In fact, it probably gives the impression that haemophilia is mainly a question of fate, and that little can be done about it. So although the game may increase knowledge, it may not encourage, and may even discourage, action to help haemophiliacs.

And now to a routine simulation. The forum could be an official committee to discuss the problems of haemophilia. The participants might have role cards representing patients, doctors, welfare agencies, blood banks, employers, charities and a representative from the finance committee of the local authority, or, if it is a national simulation, a high official in the ministry. Possibly there is some public document handed out to all the participants about the reason for calling the meeting, and what it is hoped will be achieved. The committee can have power to decide what will be done, or it can be an advisory committee. If there are large numbers of participants, several can share each role and meet as one large committee, or there could be several committees operating simultaneously. Unlike the game, the participants have considerable powers. Instead of learning information from chance cards, they learn it from each other. They feel involved. They are not players, nor are they play-actors; they are people tackling a difficult problem.

Alternatively, a routine simulation may aim to provide a structured environment in which haemophiliacs seek medical treatment. The room could be divided into areas representing the hospitals, the welfare centres and the workplaces. This is more difficult to organize than the committee simulation. It could be done by having several rounds, and in each round two chance cards are handed to each haemophiliac – one on their financial position and one on their health. Financial cards might say, 'You cannot get employment because of your health record, and you have not enough money to pay for adequate medical treatment and after-care.' A participant who is an employer might be given a card saying, 'You have decided not to employ any haemophiliac who has suffered a severe attack, and you prefer to give the jobs to people who are more reliable and who are not likely to cause such disruption and embarrassment among the workforce.' Unlike the committee simulation, the participants have little powers of choice, and possibly feel that it is just a game with chance cards and that it would be quicker and equally effective to read a pamphlet on the problems of haemophilia.

The Greenblat/Gagnon simulation uses the format of haemophiliacs seeking treatment. There are areas for doctors, blood banks, welfare agencies, but there are also areas for employers and, a nice touch this, a cemetery.

The action begins with a hurried session, limited to five minutes, during which two employers recruit workers. 'Work' consists of throwing darts at a dartboard. On being hired each worker is given a number, and when that number is called it is their turn to throw four darts. If they disregard the call because they are in a queue for medical treatment, blood or welfare, they miss their turn and do not get paid. Haemophiliacs who have had several attacks have to throw with their non-dominant hand or sitting down. The employer pays the 'wage' whatever the score, even if all four darts miss the board, but the employers' incomes depends on the total number scored by all who throw during each round. The two employers soon begin to realize that they will make more profit if they recruit only those haemophiliacs with the least severe condition. An additional source of anxiety for the haemophiliacs is an actual time limit for receiving treatment after an attack, with penalties for exceeding the limit in the form of red dots on their badges which measure the seriousness of their condition. Eight dots and they go to the cemetery.

There are two rounds and the lessons the participants learn in the first round can be applied in the second round. The officials learn how best to handle their queues, and the haemophiliacs develop their own strategies for staying alive. There are certain things they are not allowed to do, such as go and hide to avoid fate in the shape of the organizer who asks them to draw a card from a pack to indicate whether they have had an attack or not, but the participants are told that they can do anything they are not specifically forbidden to do. Thus, if they wish to lie, cheat or steal in order to stay alive (and usually several participants do take such action) then there are no 'rules' to stop them.

The last thing to be written in the simulation was the title: it is called 'Blood Money'. This simulation usually makes a profound impression on the participants. Not only does it increase their knowledge of the problems facing haemophiliacs, but it develops a sympathy for their problems which is far deeper than would be the case of the imaginary options already discussed.

One Cathy Greenblat simulation 'African Village Development Game', emerged from a training workshop in Cameroon (there were well over twenty co-authors). The subject was concerned with rural development, particularly self-help projects. The participants in the roles of the villagers had various options, including sitting back and enjoying life, or building a road. If they preferred a leisurely life, they went to part of the room provided with comforts; but if they decided to build a road they had to link together safety-pins to a specific length. During runs of this simulation, well-intentioned participants often start stringing together their safety-pins, but then give up, and retire to the comforts area, leaving the road half built, which is what can happen in real life. A routine simulation might have dealt with this by a game-like device in which the participants exchanged X number of time/labour chits for cards representing Y miles of road.

These examples will give you an idea of how feelings can be evoked by various devices – whether they be darts, safety-pins or time limits.

Lying, cheating and stealing

In creating your simulation you may have to consider law and ethics. With 'Blood Money' the participants can, if they so wish, tell lies, cheat and steal. In creating such a simulation you can either ban illegal or unethical behaviour, or allow it within certain limits. The advantage of banning it is that participants are more likely to behave within a particular code of conduct, and the disadvantage is that it is a step or two away from real life.

My own view is broadly the same as Cathy Greenblat's. I believe that participants should be allowed to do anything they are not told not to do, including unethical and illegal conduct. However, this permission is within the context of behaviour in a simulation, and that behaviour must include the acceptance of the role, including the duties and the responsibilities.

In 'Blood Money' the responsibility of the haemophiliacs is to stay alive, and if they need to cheat and steal to do so, I would not make a 'rule' to prevent them doing this. However, I would give them no protection from the consequences of their action if they were caught out by the other participants.

When I was running a prototype simulation about a literature prize set in the fictitious country of Lingua, one of the participants in the role of a publisher took me on one side and asked if it was permitted to offer a bribe to one of the judges. I replied that I didn't know, I was not in Lingua. The only rule relating to a bribe, I said, was that it had to be in Linguan money or goods, not in English money or goods.

An example of how consequences can catch up with wrong-doers comes from a transcript of a tape of 16-year-old children in West Germany participating (speaking in English) in my 'Property Trial', in which the first part was a trading session (during which some illegalities occurred), followed by a Wealth Inquiry to consider taxation and the distribution of wealth. A former witness had already described 'losing' $5,000, and the present witness is under some suspicion.

Counsel I have another question to your present wealth. Have you any houses or cars?

Witness No, no. I have selled them. I have bought from friends and . . . em . . . I bought very cheap and selled it expensive. I got much money.

Counsel Yes, I want that we think again about your methods. You are sure that they are right?

Witness Yes. [*laughter*]

Clerk I want that she comes under oath. If she takes the oath, she says 'I swear by the Almighty God that I'm telling the truth'.

Counsel Must she take the oath?

Clerk The Chairman can decide that.

Chairman You've said that you bought a house or something like that from a friend – who is that friend?

Witness Er . . . [*laughter*] I don't know.

Clerk Please say the truth.

Witness I've forgotten.

Clerk So I think we have to do that oath.

Chits and chance

When writing your simulations try to make sure that feelings arise spontaneously, and are not handed out on a chance card or a role card. But chits and counters can produce feelings, and the status of the chits can evoke different emotions as the simulation proceeds. In some cases, as in 'Starpower' by Garry Shirts, coloured wealth chits gradually become prized possessions. The grip of the hand tightens. Indifference becomes possessiveness.

Chance is sometimes a key issue when designing a simulation. To use dice or not? One aspect is whether it is a chance situation in real life. Do people have no control, partial control or complete control over the situation? A heart attack or a thunderstorm can be regarded as pure chance and can be dealt with by using dice, chance cards or some other arbitrary device. But there are simulations where the probabilities or consequences alter if a person adopts sensible eating habits or reads the weather forecast.

If, however, the situation normally depends on human decisions rather than Acts of God, then the introduction of dice is usually a confession of failure. It is almost always bad design to use chance to determine whether or not a person is carrying an umbrella, whether they spend more or less on advertizing, or whether they vote for or against the majority party.

Counters and tokens require thought. If they might be useful, take a walk round the hardware shop, toy shop, stationery counter and the department selling buttons. Think about colour coding. If some form of building takes place, consider using sticky bits of coloured paper or Lego blocks or matchsticks.

Also consider hardware. Sharpened pencils and clean notepads can make a big difference in a board-room simulation. A journalistic simulation can be greatly helped by having typewriters. If the news conference could be on television, and if your organization has video cameras, you might invite them to attend as a television camera crew, not to record a classroom event, but to get news coverage for the (fictitious) local or national broadcasting organization.

Computer-assisted simulations

Using computers in a simulation is, in my view, no different in principle from using paper and pencil, a telephone, an abacus or a typewriter. All are devices which assist communication and help tackle problems. If they are available, they can be chosen according to how well they fit into the simulated environment.

Computer programs can provide rapid results for decision-makers. This can be particularly useful in those business simulations which depend on a series of decisions based on the results of earlier decisions. Computers also have the ability to randomize numbers, thus allowing an event to be rerun without being a duplicate. Other important features of the computer are sound, graphics and word-processing facilities.

Assuming that the teacher can write computer programs or can arrange for the local school whiz-kids to do it, how can a computer assist a simulation? Obviously, if the computer is to be used as a keyboard for one student who hits the keys in silence and solves a problem without help, then (however interesting the program) this is a non-interactive simulation with possible spectator interest. If the operator thinks it is a game and if the onlookers think it is entertainment, it is not a simulation at all as there is no reality of function. However, by the same definition, a commercial game could be a simulation if the operator was not thinking of it as a point-scoring entertainment, but was trying to operate military weapons to ward off a space invasion. It would be akin to a military weapon-simulation device, or simulators used to train airline pilots. The fact that no such weaponry or space invaders existed would not affect the principle for categorizing the activity.

Suppose that a space-invasion computer game were slowed down 1000 times, or that the action was frozen altogether at certain points, and the earth strategy and tactics (and perhaps those of the aliens) were decided by group decisions, this too could have reality of function in a simulated environment on the analogy of a military-command simulation, or a TEWT – Tactical Exercise Without Troops.

As with the other devices mentioned in this chapter, the issue is whether a computer is appropriate. If the participants were journalists who had to edit news copy, or authors who had to write and edit a poem or story or article, a word processor might be entirely appropriate.

Some published computer programs, such as 'The Mary Rose', are what might be termed computer-assisted simulations and are part of what is known as computer-assisted learning (CAL). In 'The Mary Rose' the participants are groups or archaeologists and divers who try to find and excavate the Tudor ship in Portsmouth harbour. Every so often the group go back to the computer, feed in their decisions and receive the results.

I have written a simple computer program which garbles messages between earth and approaching spaceships. The garble factor decreases as the ships come closer. I have run the simulation using pencil and paper, but it takes longer to garble, and does not have the same feeling of technology. But the decision-making problems are the same – what do the messages say and what shall we do about them?

There are many articles in the literature of simulations and games on the subject of computers as the providers of models – models of an economy, a health service, storm barriers, pollution, traffic flow, queuing for meals, energy supplies, business decisions and the hazards of a mythological world. Consider two computer-assisted business simulations.

'Sixgam' produced by Pitmansoft has six groups (or individuals) each controlling a company which manufactures and sells word-processors. The simulation is played over ten rounds and the teams are given information about costs, overheads, advertising, prices, etc. They reach decisions, feed them into the computer, which calculates the number of word-processors which are sold by each team. Although the activity is usually enjoyable, there are doubts about what is actually learned – a team's success or failure may have been due not to how good they were at analysing market forces, but to whether or not they guessed a price which successfully undercut the prices set by other teams.

'Running the British Economy' (Longman) is far more am-
bitious, informative and time-consuming than 'Sixgam'.
The outcome is not influenced by other teams. No team, for
example, represents the United States economy. Participants
are given an eight-year history of the economy, which is written
in summary form and supported by a table of thirty-one
measures for each year – exports, imports, consumption ex-
penditure, aggregate demand, disposable income, etc. etc.
They then tell the computer the policy changes they wish to
make (e.g. to taxation) for that year and the computer tells
them what happened. This goes on for ten rounds (years), and
the program can be run in its basic form or with 'exogenous
shocks' – changes in world inflation rate, or a hurricane
damages North Sea oil-rigs.

I must confess to having general doubts about the educational value of most computer simulations. I don't dispute
their value for research, or for stimulating bored students, but
very often the decision-making is a game-like guesswork of
what other teams might do, or else is concentrated on discover-
ing a mathematical formula rather than an appreciation of
the context. 'Running the British Economy', which is updated every year, is better than most computer-assisted simulations for giving a real feel of the economy rather than just
number-crunching, but whether the result is worth the effort
is a matter of opinion, and clearly depends on the circumstances.

However, you can certainly look at computer simulations as
a source of ideas for writing your own non-computer simulations. And even a walk through a games arcade would
provide ideas. If you wish to use a space-invaders theme, you
could write up Space Orders, design a Space Chart, and end up
with a good interactive classroom simulation.

The same considerations apply when you look at board-
games. Examining 'Monopoly' could lead you to think about
using some of its features – for example, the fact that the
players can purchase parts of the board. In your simulation,
one group could bid for the corridor or the teacher's desk, or
produce plans for the development of the book cupboard, or

buy up all the paper and pencils. Well, it's an idea, and ideas, as distinct from published simulations, are not copyright.

Adapting, copyright and confidentiality

Should you adapt other people's simulations? It depends what you mean by adapt. It is one thing to utilize someone else's ideas (legal), but it is quite another thing to utilize someone else's documents (breach of copyright, and illegal). This book is about writing your own simulations, not about stealing other people's. But it is useful to clarify the issues, and to distinguish, as far as possible, between what is normal and acceptable practice and what is wrong, unprincipled, bad, unprofessional and against the law.

Whatever the law might be on the subject, the danger area is to move from adapting another author's materials for classroom use, to publication of such adaptations outside the classroom. The publisher of a book of poetry is unlikely to become frantic if a teacher rewrites one of the poems by changing all the place names from their originals to those of the locality of the school in order to be relevant and interesting to that particular class. But if the teacher thinks this geographically altered poem works so well that it deserves a wider audience and has it printed in the school magazine or, worse, in the local newspaper or a book, then the publisher (or author) might well start reaching for their lawyers. Even if the teacher adds the phrase 'adapted from the poem by Bloggs' or 'inspired by a poem by Bloggs' or even 'by Bloggs' this is still infringement of copyright.

It is not necessary for whole chunks of prose (poetry, music, etc.) to be copied in order to infringe copyright law. Stealing a couple of bars of music is quite sufficient grounds for a legal action.

If you copy (steal) words from other people's works, you are on very dangerous ground. If, however, you adapt the mechanics of someone's simulation or the ideas or the subject matter, that is safe and acceptable.

The law of copyright is not a barrier to authorship, it is a protection of authorship.

Some authors worry that other people will steal their works before they are published. Some are even hesitant about sending a manuscript to a publisher in case the publisher rejects the manuscript but steals the work. Fortunately, authors are protected not only by the law of copyright, but also by the law on confidentiality. In English law people are not allowed to use for their own benefit information which has been given to them in confidence. There are quite a number of legal cases involving confidentiality. One English case concerned the television series 'Rock Follies', broadcast by Thames Television in 1976 and 1977, in which the judgement was that the people involved in making the programme had, perhaps unconsciously, used ideas which had originally been given in confidence.

If you are concerned about authorship and the law – copyright, contract, royalties, subsidiary rights, etc. – you might consider joining an organization of authors. In Britain this would be the Society of Authors or the Writers' Guild.

· 4 · The first run-through

Extension of authorship

Although this book is about creating simulations, not about running simulations in the classroom, it is necessary to open the classroom door to see what happens when you try out your ideas and your documents.

The author of a simulation, unlike the author of a poem, novel or textbook, requires guinea-pigs. Simulations have to be tested, since what actually happens may be very different from what the author imagined would happen. So the first run-through can be regarded as an extension of authorship. It will provide you with practical data for assessing and altering your simulations, and it might spark off new ideas for simulation authorship. It will be a continuation of the same sort of thoughts of invention and selection which went through your mind when writing the simulation.

Probably there will be two major differences when you try out your own simulation for the first time compared with when you try out for the first time a published simulation. Firstly, you are likely to be more anxious, and perhaps more sensitive to any criticism, particularly if the guinea-pigs are teachers.

Secondly, the task itself is likely to be much easier since you know your own material thoroughly, and will have made your own guesses about the options open to the participants. Possibly you will have already tried it out, either as a complete simulation or in a shortened form, with friends, family or colleagues, or at least discussed it with your colleagues before venturing into the first public run-through.

The three traditional stages in a simulation (briefing, action, debriefing) sometimes require a preliminary stage in which you explain the simulation technique to participants who have never participated in a simulation. This chapter will examine some of the features and options of all four stages, concentrating on how they affect you as an author.

Explaining the technique

When you run a simulation, either your own or anyone else's, with a group who are generally ignorant of the simulation technique, special problems arise. In many ways, complete ignorance is best. This is easier than when they have the wrong expectations, and think that the event will be a game, or a drama, or a fun session.

If you are facing your own students and they are unfamiliar with simulations, it is likely that the simulation you have in your hand will be a well-tried and tested published simulation, not your own prototype having its first run. But if you are not so fortunate as to have your own students, or if the simulation is intended for pupils or students of a different age or on a different course, or if you try out your prototype on a teacher-training course or at a conference, you will be faced with the question – 'Do I explain the technique, and if so what do I say?'

You are now standing facing your audience, your new simulation on the table, and their eyes are upon you. You may know little or nothing about their previous experience of simulation techniques, and even if you ask a few questions like 'How many have taken part in simulations before?' the answers may not be very helpful if what they mean by a simulation is different from what you mean.

I doubt whether there is a 'right' way of doing it. I suspect that it depends a great deal on circumstances, including whether or not your simulation contains notes for participants. However, my advice is that if you are in any doubt about whether or not to explain a particular point about the technique, then don't.

At one time I used to explain that a simulation was not a game or an informal drama, etc., and give reasons and examples to illustrate the difference. This went down reasonably well if the audience were teachers, but as they knew they would be asked sooner or later to participate in a simulation, anxieties began to develop. Several teachers would ask questions – 'Could you explain the rationale of the technique?' 'What's the main point of simulations?' 'Could you please tell us how the activity relates to educational objectives?' 'Could you give us a few examples of the circumstances in which you would introduce a simulation?'

I noticed that two or three individuals often asked a series of questions. After some years of this experience, it occurred to me that many of these questions were not requests for information, but delaying tactics. The questioners were not seeking knowledge, they were seeking shelter.

Another experience was that the longer I spoke the more bewildered the audience became. Eyes began to glaze. It was as if I were reading aloud the rules of a new game, and the more rules that were read out the more confused the listeners became.

Cathy Greenblat's technique is to ask, 'Do you understand what you have to do?' In response to the chorus of 'No's', she says, 'And you are not supposed to understand at this stage; you will only understand once the action starts.'

My reaction to glazed eyes has been to reduce the explanation time from fifteen minutes to ten, from ten minutes to five, and sometimes a nil explanation – just divide them up, tell them the approximate time limits, hand out the documents, and let them get on with it as best they may. If the simulation is any good, the nature of the activity will soon be apparent, particularly if there are notes for participants. And the teachers may be impressed afterwards that the simulation generated a great deal of activity with almost no time spent in preliminary explanations.

I now almost always say, 'If you have any queries at all, don't ask me, ask the people in your own group. If it is an important point and none of you know, then come and ask me.'

However, there is a special difficulty when inexperienced participants are teachers. Teachers, by training, assess materials. But if, during the action part of the simulation, they mentally assess the educational merits of the materials, they have stepped outside their roles. And if they actually say aloud, 'This activity might go down well (badly) with my students', they are causing the other participants to abandon their roles if they respond to the remarks. So with teachers I usually plead with them not to think or speak like teachers during the course of the simulation, but to involve themselves fully in their roles, responsibilities, duties and problems, and leave all assessment until afterwards. Although this plea may not prevent the occasional intrusive thoughts of assessment, it is usually sufficient to prevent the teachers from jerking other participants out of the simulation by making verbal assessments during the course of the action.

The only other point I sometimes emphasize to any group of inexperienced participants is that acceptance of the role means that they must not be magicians or gods. They cannot invent 'facts' to win arguments. If, for example, I am introducing an international-affairs simulation, I always explain that they have full power to negotiate, take diplomatic initiatives, give news conferences, but if they issue orders to anyone outside the event, I decide whether that order was obeyed, and what happened outside the classroom. I warn them that if they order a bombing raid or a day of prayer then the result is outside their control, and what happens may not be what they anticipated. This warning is usually enough to prevent the simulation degenerating into what I call a Magical Escalation Game – 'I've put 100,000 soldiers along your frontier,' 'And I've just put a million soldiers on your frontier,' 'My Air Force has just bombed your air bases,' 'No, they haven't; they have all been shot down, but my Air Force has blasted the whole of your country with nuclear bombs,' 'No, it hasn't, because my agents captured you before you could give the order, and so you're dead,' 'No, I'm not, because. . . .'

The briefing

You created the simulation, so there is no problem about the briefing being inadequate because you didn't read the materials properly. The danger is likely to be that you can't see the wood for the trees. This, coupled with any anxieties about the outcome, may lead you to make a long, rambling and nervous verbal introduction. Not only might you be tempted to explain too many facts, you may also be so keen for your simulation to succeed that you spell out too many options, and suggest to the participants the most sensible course of action.

While you were actually devising and writing the materials you may have been very conscious of the desirability to confer as much decision-making power as possible on the participants, but when you introduce your own creative effort there is a real danger that your behaviour may be far from consistent with this aim.

Even before the action starts you may have allocated the brightest students to the key roles, and made sure that the easiest or most interesting roles were given to the persistent trouble-makers. You might be all too well aware of the way in which particular students sit together and refuse to be parted, and who behave as if they owned the chairs in which they sit. You may know full well that X is hostile to Y, and that Z is unlikely to make any contribution to any activity whatsoever.

But this bleak picture should not apply. If they are your own students then they should have participated in a simulation before and will be aware that chair-ownership does not count, and that groups mix and move according to roles and the flow of events. If they are someone else's students (or teachers), simply allocate roles by random procedures. If you like, you can ask the participants if they object, and there is a good chance that they will not only not object, but will positively welcome it.

However, if you are worried about a key role being filled by participant X, then what you can do quite legitimately is to give two people that role, and still allocate the roles at random. In that way the two participants can work together, help each other out, and back each other up.

Having made provision, if required, for doubling up key roles, what remains of the objection to random role allocation? If you look at it objectively, you may conclude that it is mainly your own desire for a favourable result. You wish to give your own simulation the best possible chance on its first run-through, and therefore decide to load the dice. The advice I tend to give is that the author should examine the problem calmly in advance of the event. Meditate on the fact that a simulation is not a guided exercise or a rehearsed event. The justification for a simulation is not that the 'result' is 'right', or that the 'performances' are 'good'. On the contrary, people learn from their mistakes. In a simulation, mistakes are not only inevitable, they are desirable. Not only does a simulation have a debriefing when these things can be discussed, but individual participants conduct their own private debriefings which may occur a day or a week or a month after the event.

Just as you might explain to the participants that they are not going to be criticized because they 'got it wrong', so you could explain to yourself that you will not be criticized if the event fails to achieve a 'good' result. The authorship of the materials belongs to you, but the event belongs to the participants. Naturally, the temptations to manipulate can be considerable. Your colleagues may want to know what happened, and you wish to avoid having to say, 'The participants did not reach any conclusions and never got round to discussing the key issue.' But it makes sense for you to be brave and support your own authorship. You want to see how it runs as a simulation, and if you change it into a guided exercise then you have missed the point.

If you are convinced that random allocation of roles is a good thing, but think the participants may object, then ask them.

Explain that it will give them all the same chance. Put the question to them a day or two before the event begins, and let them decide.

Various devices can be used for randomness. If there are two groups, you can go round the class numbering them in turn – one, two, one, two – and asking the number ones to go to the corner near the window and the number twos to the table near the door. Another way is to lay the role cards face down on the table and let the students pick. With unequal groups you could number all the participants from one to six and announce, 'I'll roll this dice and the first number to come up will be the journalist(s), the next number will be the trade union leader(s) and everyone else will be ordinary trade union members.' I have used all these methods, plus toothpicks with one 'short straw' where the participant who draws the short stick is the shop steward, etc. On some occasions groups themselves have asked for the sticks or the dice to allocate roles randomly within their group – who should be secretary, who should be the radio announcer, who should be the interviewer.

The action

Once the action has begun, any anxiety about whether the event will 'succeed' or 'fail' may tempt you to sit down next to the participants and say, 'How are you getting on? Do you understand the documents? Have you thought of all the options?' Don't. It is likely to distract them, and make them nervous. Sit back and relax, or mark the class register, or even go for a cup of coffee. Disengagement on your part will convince them that they are in charge, and that they do not need, nor will they receive, your help and guidance.

If they ask you any questions, then pause for a few moments before you answer. Categorize the question. Is it about (1) the mechanics of the simulation, or (2) the facts within the simulation, or is it (3) a request for advice about policy? From the point of view of running the simulation, then answer the question according to the category.

1 If it is about the mechanics ('How much more time have we got?') give the information required.
2 If it is a question about facts ('Is Orangeland a democracy?') evade the question if the answer is in the documents, and if it is not in the documents then give a plausible answer.
3 If it is on policy ('Would it be a good idea if we went north?') then explain that you don't know, you are not there, or that you are only the organizer.

From the point of view of authorship, make a note of these questions, and at what stage in the simulation they were asked. You could even use a tape-recorder if the participants are unlikely to be distracted by this. The why and the when of these questions can be of great value in assessing the event afterwards.

You will have plenty of time to walk around, but you should do so slowly and unobtrusively, and gaze into the distance. You can notice things out of the corners of your eye, and you can listen. Try to avoid giving smiles or frowns.

Whether you walk, stand or sit, notice where the heads are, and which way they are facing. Are they together? Is one head well apart from the others, and has that participant dropped out from the activity? Observe who is doing what, and who speaks and who doesn't.

My own assessment of prototype simulations depends a great deal on how many people involve themselves in the activity. If only three or four people do the talking in a group of half a dozen or more, I take this as a sign that the simulation needs altering in some way. But if all, or almost all, of the participants take an active part one way or another, I am fairly satisfied, even if the actual decisions made are utterly disastrous.

When observing your simulation, you don't have to see and hear everything. What matters is what is going on in the heads of the participants, and they can tell you that afterwards.

What happens if someone misbehaves? What if the Prime Minister kicks the Foreign Secretary on the ankle, or if one of the Councillors knocks the reporter to the ground? What

matters is that you should assess the situation correctly. Basic-
ally, there is no such thing as misbehaviour in a simulation;
what has happened is that the simulation has ended for those
involved. They have abandoned their roles, reverted to being
students (or children) and started a private war. Undoubtedly
the best way to tackle this is within the plausibility of the
simulation. Send a message to the person or persons involved
that they are wanted for an urgent conference or telephone call.
When you have extracted them find out what the problem is. It
may be that X has a headache, or that Y has insulted Z's
girlfriend at a disco dance. The remedy may be a change of
roles, or perhaps you could ask the person to help you to run
the simulation.

It may be, of course, that the misbehaviour is related to your
authorship. If one person has nothing to do except watch the
others busily enjoying themselves, the result may be boredom,
followed by indignation, followed by sabotage.

If your simulation involves heated emotions, and if the old
age pensioner strikes the wicked landlord, this is not misbehaviour in the way I have been using the word. In this case there
is no abandonment of role − in fact there is a tremendous
involvement in the role. From the point of view of authorship,
you should take another look at your documents. From your
point of view as organizer, the immediate problem is the
landlord who is now sitting on the floor dabbing a bleeding
nose. You could take on the role of ambulance man or police-
man, since you are clearly dealing with an emergency, and this
might be one of the few cases where an organizer is justified in
taking a role.

The debriefing

If it is at all possible, I like to make a debriefing (the follow-up,
the discussion) a continuation of the simulation. So instead of
the participants reverting immediately to pupil–student status,
with you immediately becoming the teacher, you could try to
set up an extended event involving evaluation of what has just
happened.

If your simulation involves groups, ask them to remain in their groups but to sit in a circle, or face each other in parallel lines, or form a triangle or square, depending on the number of groups.

I usually ask them to take it in turn to explain what their problems were, and how they tackled them. This can be given plausibility by asking them to imagine that they are reporting back to their leaders, or explaining their case to a tribunal, or simply informing their subordinates (shareholders, members) what they have done.

This has the advantage of continuing the practice of language and communication skills, and perhaps organizational skills if the group arrange that one person shall make one point and another person another. Also it puts everyone in the picture; they can all be informed of what is on someone else's role card or in the private facsimile documents.

Doing it this way will help you as an author gain an insight into how they saw your simulation from the inside. If in the debriefing they immediately revert to student status, their comments are less spontaneous and are likely to be cautious and generalized.

Once the participants have explained what they did and why, a general discussion can follow. Most published simulations give you a list of questions you can raise in the debriefing and this often gives the impression that you must be in charge. But it is worth considering, preferably before you introduce the simulation, whether or not you can ask the participants to take charge of the follow-up. My advice would be to put them in charge, but make sure they had enough time and facilities to organize themselves properly.

However, you will certainly have some questions you wish to ask from the point of view of authorship. 'Did the documents contain too much information or too little? Were key facts missing? Could the areas of decision-making be expanded?'

Naturally, you don't have to agree to all, or indeed any, of their suggestions, but they are your first group of guinea-pigs, and their comments should be of considerable help.

Assessing and categorizing what happened

Whatever the category or type of simulation you have created, the principles of assessing the whole event from the point of view of an author are very similar, and might be summarized as follows:

1 *Was the behaviour consistent with participant power?*

Did the participants react to the briefing and the documents in a way which showed that they were in charge of events, or did they behave as if they were counters being pushed around a board? Did they behave like stereotypes and play-act, or did they deal with the problem in a sensible and rational way?

2 *To what extent did the participants have reality of function?*

How real were their powers, responsibilities and duties when compared to the real world? Did they say, 'Our memo from the managing director', or did they say, 'This piece of paper'? If the atmosphere was a formal occasion, did they refer to each other as 'Councillor Atkinson' and 'Lord Mayor', or did they address each other by their own first names?

3 *Did the event flow smoothly?*

Did the participants keep turning to you and asking, 'What are we supposed to do now?' Were there times when individuals or groups pulled out their newspapers or comics, or was everyone interested in what was going on even though they themselves might not have been saying something or doing something at that particular moment?

4 *What events occurred which you did not expect?*

What initiatives were shown by individuals and groups that you had not envisaged? Were there demands to know specific 'facts' which were not included in the documents? Did the unexpected events indicate a strength or a weakness in the simulation?

Apart from observing what went on, and discussing this in the debriefing, there are several other ways of gaining information.

One method is to use a questionnaire. This is a favourite research technique among pioneers of simulations, but I rather suspect that this may have been due to a desire to give statistical weight to a judgement that simulations are educationally valuable. One often finds that the questions float in the air. Participants might be asked, 'Did you find it (a) enjoyable, (b) mildly interesting, or (c) rather boring?' But what is the activity being compared with? Is it enjoyable compared with filling in an income tax form or with playing football? In any case, the number of participants may be too small to assess the validity of the results of the questionnaire.

Even with large numbers there is the problem of interpreting the findings of a questionnaire. I remember the mass of statistics compiled from a questionnaire on a large-scale simulation which involved well over a hundred participants representing government, trade unions, employers and agencies including the Arbitration and Conciliation Service. The authors found that three people indicated that the simulation was boring and a waste of time, and the authors concluded that this was not surprising since in any simulation there were always one or two who do not seem to get much out of it. However, when I talked to the authors it turned out that all three participants had been members of the Arbitration and Conciliation Service, and that no one had called on their services. They had sat there for three or four hours doing virtually nothing except talk among themselves and observe how busy other participants were. So their response to the questionnaire was not a criticism of simulations, it was a complaint that they had not been allowed to participate.

The part of questionnaires which I find useful is that devoted to the open-ended type of question – 'What did you like most (least) and why?' The answer has the disadvantage to the researcher that it does not easily fit into a table of numbers, but it does provide useful information to the author, and if you can follow it up with an interview with the person who gave the answers then you may be rewarded with specific ideas, not just vague conclusions.

My own preference is the interview. Then I can follow up immediately the points that are being made. I can ask for examples, and pose hypothetical questions – 'What would you have done if . . . ?' In chapter 2, 'Getting started', I gave an excerpt from a taped interview I had with a 14-year-old girl, and this illustrates how points can emerge which would otherwise remain buried. She made the suggestion that there might be a simulation about seat belts, but followed it up immediately with the remark, 'You couldn't do much of a simulation on that, could you?' If this suggestion had been made in a group discussion, it almost certainly would have starved to death through lack of interest while others put forward suggestions about simulations on drugs, murders or pop music. In an interview one can deliberately go down what at first appears to be a dead-end, and the exploration can be rewarding.

· 5 · Rewriting

Reasons for rewriting

A good run-through does not necessarily mean that nothing can be improved, nor does a poor run-through mean that everything must be changed.

Before starting to rewrite it is helpful to sit back and try to survey the whole concept of your simulation, because if you start by tinkering with one document, you may find that this requires you to change several other documents in order to be consistent, and the total sum of the changes may not be beneficial.

A useful starting-point might be the four categories of assessment mentioned in the last chapter, which covered (1) participant power, (2) reality of function, (3) a smooth flow, and (4) unexpected events.

Obviously there are plenty of other criteria you could use, but the first two cover the question of whether the event is a simulation, the third is whether it works well, and the fourth point is included in case you might miss something important. It is fairly common for an author to concentrate on watching whether the simulation achieves its stated aims, and to fail to notice achievements which were not part of the aims.

In rewriting your simulation there may be opportunities for improvement by changing the concepts. For example, part of the briefing might be incorporated into the action, and so might the debriefing. And although this chapter is concerned with changes in your prototype simulation, several examples are relevant for transforming a case study (project, game) into a simulation.

Authors often find that a simple simulation works well, and believe that if it were expanded it would be even better. Bigger is not necessarily better. Also the process of adding more facts, roles, film strips, explanatory booklets and so forth can turn the simulation into a fact-learning exercise. There is nothing wrong with this if that is the intention, but what often happens is that the result is neither one thing nor another, but consists of documents which lead to an unhappy muddled mish-mash activity.

However, a common mistake is that the first version is too complicated. In the first run-through the participants may have floundered in a mass of documents, there may have been too many unemployed participants waiting for something to happen, and the procedures may have been too cumbersome for tackling the problems.

If you want a complicated simulation in order to challenge the participants and give them practice in coping with a mass of data, that is fine, but if you are aiming at a simulation which fits neatly into an hour, your two aims are incompatible.

If your simulation needs simplification, the sort of questions to ask yourself are, 'Is this document necessary?' 'Can one long document be simplified into two short ones?' 'Are these particular facts relevant for the action?' 'Can this explanatory document be made simpler and more interesting by incorporating it into a facsimile-type document?'

The rest of this chapter will consist of examples of rewriting which has been done, or which could be done, to some published simulations, plus a few illustrations of why and how I rewrite some of my own simulations. Most of the examples have been referred to in previous chapters, though not in the context of rewriting.

'Starpower'

This is almost certainly the best known of all simulations. It is the brainchild of Garry Shirts, and the way he rewrote it has probably had a more profound effect on the history of simulations than any other single event. The rewriting had the effect of removing stereotype roles, and introducing a concept of – it is difficult to condense what I mean into one word – abstraction.

When I met Garry Shirts in California, he explained that 'Starpower' began life as a routine confrontation simulation between blacks and whites. He described the run-through – all the participants were white, but the 'blacks' jumped on the tables and demanded equal rights and an abolition of racial prejudice. Everyone, he said, was very pleased with the result. They felt that the experience had been really worthwhile. But Garry Shirts had been disgusted by what happened. In his view the participants had been play-acting. They had thought that they had entered into the 'black experience', but they had leapt into cardboard stereotypes.

It was while driving a car from San Diego to Palm Springs that Shirts redesigned 'Starpower'. Instead of racial conflict, Shirts thought of the idea of transforming the concept into a trading situation in which there were neutrally named groups – Squares, Circles and Triangles – who started the simulation with unequal wealth. There was a certain amount of promotion and demotion from group to group, but this was engineered at the start and was not the result of trading skills. Then, out of the blue, the organizer gives the top group, the Squares, the right to change the trading rules if they so wish.

By deprejudicing the concepts – Triangles rather than blacks, Squares rather than whites – the participants cannot blame the world for their actions. They cannot tell the organizer afterwards, 'I don't normally behave like that, I was just imitating racist behaviour, which is what I thought you wanted us to do.' Instead, the situation has become transformed. Shirts himself says that an author may wish to 'distort and redefine' in order to shed a new light on familiar facts (Shirts 1975).

In 'Starpower', real fights sometimes take place, not between young delinquents but among college lecturers. The organizer sometimes has to step in quite quickly once fists clench. Usually there is no violence, but there is discontent, apathy, smugness, contempt, pride, protest and revolution. Even if the Squares decide to use their power to give money to the Triangles, this is rarely accepted with gratitude, and is sometimes rejected with rudeness.

Shirts distorted reality into an abstract event, a situation without geography or time. The event could be occurring in a distant galaxy, or in the future, or in some long-forgotten historical backwater. It is like a play without scenery, in which people, with their motives, virtues and vices, loom large. It highlights the personalities, the prejudices, greed or altruism of those taking part. For many people, the experience proves to be an unexpected insight into their own personalities.

Naturally, we can't all be Garry Shirts. But the example does show the value of rethinking the concepts, of exploring options, of getting away from the idea that simulations should be models of reality, or overloaded with facts, or conceived as if they were a sort of railway track with the organizer pulling the switch points to get the train to a predetermined destination. It is also an example of the importance of the author assessing the results of a run-through as it affects the whole simulation, not just individual parts.

'Tenement'

As we saw earlier, this simulation provokes emotions, but unlike 'Starpower' they tend to be built in, thus reducing the spontaneity of behaviour and introducing play-acting, particularly in relations between landlord and tenants.

However, the latest version, published in 1980, is a rewrite of the 1972 version, and some of the changes are instructive. The first version included a role for a Rent Tribunal, and the role card said, 'Remember, it is important to get all the facts. The tenant and landlord may tell different stories and the Tribunal will have to decide which one is nearer the truth.'

But as the other documents lacked key facts, the task of the Rent Tribunal was impossible. For example, the Rent Tribunal's card said that a notice to quit may be given in writing, or else verbally in front of witnesses, in order to be valid. So the Tribunal would almost certainly ask, 'Was this done?' The question would bewilder both the landlord and the family facing eviction. They wouldn't know the answer. They could step outside the simulation and say, 'I don't have any information about that on my card', or they could make up the answer. The landlord might say that the eviction was given verbally before witnesses, and the family would presumably deny this. So what does the Rent Tribunal do about its important job 'to get all the facts'? Perhaps it decides in favour of the most convincing liar.

In the latest version the Rent Tribunal has been abandoned, and replaced by 'the Rent Officer'. This omits any mention of notices to quit, and refers to ways of counting rooms to help assess a 'fair rent' and suggests that the Rent Officer should arrange a meeting with landlord and tenant. This is a simpler and more positive version of the original role card.

In the original version there was a role for a Hartwell family whose role card said that they complained to the Health Department about the deplorable conditions, but nothing was done, except that the landlord increased the Hartwell's rent by £2 to discourage them from making further complaints. If the family went to the Citizens' Advice Bureau and gave them this information, and the Citizens' Advice Bureau contacted the local health authorities and asked why nothing had been done in the Hartwell case, the answer would be a deafening silence – the authorities know nothing about it. Thus another key fact is missing, leaving the participants floundering around trying to rescue themselves (and the simulation) from allegations of lying or incompetence or corruption.

In the latest version there is no Hartwell family. What was their flat is now empty.

'Spring Green Motorway'

Earlier, we examined some of the problems of the role cards in this simulation, particularly from the viewpoint of implanting personalities and of not including some important facts. The discussion was based on a rewritten version published in 1980; the earlier version dates from 1971. But unlike the rewrite of 'Tenement', most of the changes are not improvements.

The old version of the motorway controversy contained no caricatures on the backs of role cards, as does the 1980 version. And as the new version includes film strips and more information about motorways and the environment, this rather suggests that one aim was to produce a bigger and better version.

Compare the original version of June Finlay's role card with the rewritten role card which we examined in chapter 3.

1971

> **Miss June Finlay**. You are a reporter on the staff of the Ildridge Gazette. You used to work in London, but now you enjoy newly married life in the country.

1980

> **Ms June Finlay**. You are a young, talented reporter on the Ildridge Gazette. You used to work in London but gave up possible promotion to move to the country which you love. You know that the Department of Transport have offered to pay Lord Smirk £100,000 for this land and intend to raise the point at the public meeting.

The first version contains an interesting inconsistency. The title 'Miss' is inconsistent with the information that she is married. This mistake presumably arose because of rewritings prior to the first publication, and the authors forgot that a change in one place can require changes elsewhere. The mistake is corrected in the 1980 version when the character becomes 'Ms'. But otherwise the shorter role card is superior to the rewritten version. It is reasonably concise and it concentrates on function, apart from (1) the sex casting of the role, (2) the strange reference to having worked in London, and (3) the irrelevant information about being married. However, there is no problem for the participant about what to do – the task is to report the meeting for the Ildridge Gazette.

In the rewritten version two adjectives have been inserted – 'young' and 'talented' – which invite play-acting. In fact, 'talented', which may have been inserted to reassure the participant that 'she' is more than capable of doing the job, may have the reverse effect. An anxious participant might think, 'I have never done any reporting, so how on earth can I play a talented reporter?' The result may be a stereotype piece of play-acting based on a Hollywood movie.

The later version talks about 'the country which you love' and the participant might decide that this has been inserted for a purpose – to bias the reporter against the motorway.

In a real situation even the most junior of reporters would have checked out the story of Lord Smirk's £100,000 before the meeting began, and they would certainly know the source of the information. As reporters do not ask questions at public meetings (they ask questions before or after) this means that any participant in the role who knows anything about newspaper reporting faces a curious dilemma. It opens up the possibility that Ms June Finlay is not talented at all (she was not promoted in London and is evidently not a chief reporter in Ildridge), and so she may be an inefficient, self-opinionated conservationist. This opinion is supported to some extent by the illustration of what she looks like on the back of her role card.

The inconsistencies in this role card and in other aspects of the rewritten version suggest that this is another example of tackling documents in a piecemeal manner rather than having an overall concept about what is supposed to be happening in the simulation. For a much fuller examination of the rewriting of this simulation, the reader should refer to the article by Rex

MS JUNE FINLAY

Walford, 'Spring Green Motorway: A question of reconstruction' (1983).

'Terry Parker'

An example of differences between a role-play activity and a simulation can be seen by examining the design of 'Terry Parker', published by Community Service Volunteers. Although it is described on the cover as 'a simulation', it is predominantly role-play with a few simulation elements. There are five role cards – for Terry Parker's probation officer, mother, teacher, headmaster and girlfriend. Those for his probation officer and his mother are shown on p. 90.

The rest of the class becomes a group (or groups) with the function of a committee of wardens and governors of Beechwood, which is the name of the children's home where Terry Parker lives. All participants, including the role-players, have

1 William Adams – Probation Officer

Terry has been on probation for 6 months, after being involved with a group of boys who took and drove away a car. He has also been under a Care Order of the local Council, as being out of the control of his mother. He is a quiet and pleasant boy by himself, and has kept out of trouble since, and you feel he is easily led by other people. He does seem to have a chip on his shoulder about being 'hard done by'.

2 Sandra Parker – Mother

You have never had much control over Terry – he has lacked a father's firm hand and always gone his own way, even when he was at junior school. Your husband left home when Terry was 5, and neither of you have seen him since. Terry cannot remember him, although sometimes he talks as if he does. When he comes home from Beechwood at weekends he seems pleased to see you at first, but by Sunday he is off the rails again, shouting, swearing and smoking.

the same background sheet giving facts about Terry's history of delinquency and the options available. The five role-players are interviewed one after the other by the committee, which then makes a recommendation (in the form of advice to the social services department) about Terry's future. Two points can be noted about the design and the documents.

1 Key facts are missing

There is no information which distinguishes the responsibilities of the wardens from the governors. Neither group has any private document. There is no information at all about how Terry has behaved during his year at Beechwood.

2 The role-players have no decision-making powers

None of the five role-players, even the officials, are members of the committee and have no task other than to provide information (real or invented) to the committee. They have nothing to do before or after being interviewed individually.

In the running of this event the five role-players might well take advantage of their brief spell on the stage by hamming it up. The committee may not feel personally involved in what happened to Terry at Beechwood, and so they may detach themselves from the role and behave as if they were students examining a case study. Alternatively, they might be disappointed by the lack of key facts, and remedy the omission by inventing some fun facts of their own, and play-acting generally.

To turn an activity like this into a simulation would not be difficult. Those role-players who could plausibly be on the committee, if only in an advisory capacity (probation officer, headmaster or even mother) could be retained, the other roles abolished and any relevant information transferred to suitable documents.

Instead of having a background sheet, there could be one document for the governors dealing with general policy, and one for the wardens dealing with how Terry behaved at Beechwood. These documents (or a separate facsimile document) could state who has the final say in Terry's future in the event of disagreement – the governors, the wardens, or a vote of the whole committee?

The information in the background sheet relating to the three options, (1) a juvenile court supervision order, (2) continuing the care order, or (3) returning Terry to his home, could be contained in a short legalistic document available to all members of the committee, either on the table or in a 'library'.

The effect of this rewriting would be to make the event fully participatory. The part-time roles would go, and the wardens and the governors would have to explain different things to each other, and perhaps argue the matter from different viewpoints.

'We're Not Going to Use Simulations'

This simulation began life as an article entitled 'Introducing Simulations', which I wrote for *Practical English Teaching*. It was simply an illustration of a simulation about teaching and about simulations. I wrote no documents, but just outlined the idea. Some months later I saw an advertisement for a competition organized by the English Speaking Union about ideas or materials which could be used in the teaching of English as a foreign language. So I wrote the documents, and sent the simulation in, and it won a prize. At this stage it had never been tried out, nor did I feel it was worth bothering about since I saw no chance of publication. What pushed the simulation into the rewrite stage was that the publishers of my book *Simulations in Language Teaching* asked me to include a complete simulation as an appendix. So I tried out the simulation with half a dozen different groups, including secondary-school teachers, administrators and teachers of English from European countries who were in England on a course. Fortunately, there was not much to rewrite. The basic concept worked, and all I did was to simplify some of the individual role cards and reshape the notes for the organizer. As mentioned earlier, I later tried it out with 14-year-olds and it worked, but this was probably because they had already been involved in several simulations. So I rewrote it by reducing three of the four official documents to one, and keeping the document about the Zed Incident and the six role cards virtually unchanged. I renamed it 'Simulations Out'. This example shows how chance events can influence authorship, and one bit of writing can lead to another bit. In fact, a few weeks after writing the imaginary dialogues for the castle-designing simulation and the one about the mountain/plainspeople, I decided to see if I could produce a couple of simulations based on these ideas. The first became 'Fort' and the second became 'The Year of the Dove'.

'Radio Covingham'

It is important to realize that writing and rewriting of documents (notes, diagrams, resolutions) often occurs spontaneously within a simulation and is carried out by the participants. Just as the final version of your own documents may not reveal the amount of effort that has gone into them, so too the documents produced within a simulation may reveal only a small part of the communication skills involved.

An example of this occurs in 'Radio Covingham', in which the participants are radio journalists who have to produce a ten-minute programme entitled *News and Views at Seven* from given materials. The news items flow in gradually during the course of the simulation, and one of them entitled 'Poison' was deliberately badly written.

Davis, Haswell   POISON

   Police cars went through the streets of Haswell this morning. The cars had loud speakers. The loud speakers were used to give a message to the people of Haswell. The message asked the people of Haswell to be on the lookout for any small green bottles. The people of Haswell were told that the bottles contained poison.
   The police message said that the bottles had been dumped on a rubbish tip in Durton Road. The people of Haswell were asked to warn their children not to play with any of these bottles or open them. The bottles should be handed in to the police. The police cars went through Haswell giving this message to the people so as to warn them of the danger of poison.

SENT 1350 LHU

A group of 14-year-olds at a north London comprehensive school rewrote this item as follows:

Police cars went through the streets of Haswell looking for small green bottles containing poison. People in Haswell were told by loud-speakers that the bottles had been dumped on a local rubbish-tip. Parents were told to keep their children away from the dump. People in Haswell who find any sort of green bottles should inform the police at once.

Here is a transcript from tape of part of the discussion which had gone on among this particular group of children in rewriting this news item:

Read that out and give it over to me.
Police cars went through the streets of Haswell looking for small . . .
What? What's that?

It doesn't matter 'cos you're not going to read it.
Yes, but we want to look at it.
Looking for what?
Small green bottles containing poison.
How do you spell 'containing'?
C.o.n.t.a.i.n.ing.
Right. Containing. No, that'll need a bit of changing.
People in Haswell were, not was. People in Haswell were told . . .
Were told by loud-speakers . . . right.
People were told to keep . . .
No. Parents were told to keep.
Right. Parents were told to keep their children away from the dump.
People in Haswell who find any poison . . . poison?
Any small green bottles.
Or any green bottles.
Any sort of green bottles.
OK. Who find any sort of green bottles to hand them in to the police.
Not hand in.
No, should tell the police.
No, inform the police.
How do you spell 'inform'?
I.n.f.o.r.m. No, not m. in. in. inform.
OK. You just write it out and I'll copy it out.

This particular simulation does allow a certain amount of invention of corroborative facts, since the teams of journalists are allowed to interview each other as people who might be connected with news items, or with the other documents. Here is another example of how a group of 14-year-old girls in a comprehensive school in the East End of London used three of their group for this item – announcer, interviewer, interviewee.

Announcer This is a warning to people who are living in the Haswell area that they should watch out for many small green bottles that have been found containing dangerous chemicals. Police have found many bottles dumped on a rubbish-tip in a nearby street. We now interview a mother who has lost her child to these dangerous chemicals. Over to Miss Jane Green.

Jane Thanks, Jo. Mrs Smith, thanks for coming along to the studio to talk to us. We understand how you must be feeling. We are very sorry about the loss of your child. Can you say something about exactly what happened to cause your son's death?

Mrs Smith Yesterday afternoon my son was playing on the estate when a boy friend of his threw a bottle at him. It is believed to have smashed on his shoulder and the chemical had gone in his face. The police came to my house to tell me that I had lost my son.

Jane Thank you, Mrs Smith. Back to you, Jo.

Announcer So this is a warning to parents who live nearby to keep their children safe.

It can be difficult to draw a precise line between legitimate inference from the documents on the one hand, and invention of facts to win arguments or sensationalize events on the other. However, by inventing the death of one of the children these 14-year-old girls seem to have gone beyond fair inference. Had such a death occurred, it would have been reported in the news documents. But this example of over-invention is not in itself a reason for rewriting the document 'Poison' and including the information that no one (yet) had died. The poison was dangerous and someone could have died between the reporter phoning the story to the radio station and the item being broadcast. The important document in this case is notes for participants, and the second paragraph states:

What you can do and what you can't do.

You can rewrite the material, but you can't invent news.

You can interview members of your own team in various roles, say as someone who wrote a letter, or is connected with a handout or the news items, but only in connection with the material.

The excluded middle

The examples given so far in this chapter have concentrated on the rewriting of documents because of inconsistencies, play-acting and the omission of key facts.

A more difficult concept is what I call the excluded middle, which is not the same as the omission of key facts. An excluded middle is a question-mark in the centre of the action where the author has deliberately (or by accident) left a gap for imaginative decision-making and has not spelt out all the main arguments and all the main options of behaviour. The excluded middle is probably the best part of the simulation, and it often marks the difference between a good imaginative simulation and a dull one. The gap enhances the powers of the participants by giving them scope to tackle their problems, rather than confining them to discussion of the pros and cons of a given list of arguments and options.

One of the subtle dangers during the course of your rewriting is that you may have been so impressed by the arguments or actions of some of the participants in the run-through that you write these into the documents, thus filling in the excluded middle.

Here are some examples of excluded middles, and how inexperienced authors might have had the holes filled in.

'Starpower'

When the Squares are told that they now have the power to change the trading rules if they wish, they are not advised how to do it, or whether to do it. The Circles and Triangles are given no hints about how they might react to this. It would have been very easy for Garry Shirts to have written role cards to deal with these options.

An over-helpful author might have written:

Triangles You have the least amount of wealth. You may, if you wish, ask for a meeting of all groups to consider the situation, or you can decide within your own group what to do, or you can each take individual action.

Circles: You do not have as much wealth as the Squares, but you have more wealth than the Triangles. You should try to preserve your wealth at all costs. Consult with the Squares and ask them to take account of your position, and if they refuse then consider making an alliance with the Triangles.

Squares: You have more wealth than the Circles, and a great deal more than the Triangles. The Triangles are likely to be very annoyed that you have been given the power to change the trading rules, so it might be useful to offer some of your wealth to the Triangles in order that you can ensure that the trading system will continue to operate in your favour.

Note that despite the 'you can' and 'if you wish' phrases, these additional role cards manipulate, or at least attempt to manipulate, the behaviour of the participants.

'Talking Rocks'

There are no role cards for the participants. The situation is explained to them by the organizer, and they are simply told they must not use modern symbols in their drawings, nor write any words or letters as they have no written language.

Vernon, who said he received a good deal of help from Garry Shirts, could have written role cards for various groups to help them:

Nomad Group A: When drawing your pictures it is a good idea to remember that the sun rises in the east and sets in the west. This may help you to show which direction you want other nomad groups to take in order to find good pasture.

Nomad Group B: There are lots of ways in which you might draw good pasture or bad pasture. A good pasture might have fat sheep on it, and a poor pasture might have thin sheep or dead sheep.

Nomad Group C: Nomads walk with their sheep, and this may give you an idea about what to draw to show where the route begins and where it ends. Or, instead of drawing nomads or sheep, there is nothing to stop you drawing footprints.

The participants would have been helped even more had all this information been contained in a single document. By not helping the participants Vernon not only ensured that what happened related to the inventiveness of the participants, but also created a developmental aspect in which good ideas are gradually picked up by other groups and poor ideas are dropped. One of the fascinating aspects of 'Talking Rocks' is the evolution of a 'language', something which would have emerged almost readymade if the hole in the middle had been filled in.

'Terry Parker'

Although this was more role-play and case study than a simulation, it has one interesting missing element – Terry Parker himself. It would have been extremely easy to write such a role card. 'I know I've not co-operated, but. . . .' And if Terry Parker had been present, the event might have ended quite quickly. 'Will you really do your best to reform?' 'Yes, I will.' 'Good, so we'll recommend that you can go home.' 'Thanks.' 'We've finished now, Sir.'

'Blood Money'

Although the role cards explain procedures about how much is earned by throwing darts, and how much can be given in welfare aid, etc., there is no advice on how to deal with the problems that inevitably crop up. Cathy Greenblat could have made the simulation run in the 'right' direction by feeding advice into the role cards.

Employers: Before you employ people it is a good idea to check their likely benefit to you as employees. If they have to sit down when they throw, or use the non-dominant hand, or if they are frequently absent, then your profits will fall and you might go bankrupt.

Doctors: You will find that you receive a good deal of money from your patients, so that might help you in dealing with the queue of people wanting your services. You might consider using some of this money to employ someone as a nurse or secretary to help deal with the more severe cases of haemophilia.

Had such advice been introduced, the employers would undoubtedly have made higher profits and the cemetery would have had fewer bodies, but the point of the simulation would have been lost. Instead of the participants feeling the emotions of tackling the difficulties without advice, they would have merely rationalized their procedures along the lines suggested, and avoided the emotions.

'We're Not Going to Use Simulations'

When I wrote the role cards for the three teachers and the three inspectors I deliberately left a hole in the middle. The role cards of the teachers deal with the conditions in Blue School, but nothing about what a simulation is. The inspectors have role cards dealing with the definition of a simulation, but nothing about conditions at Blue School. The Ministry's regulations are ambiguous. The key sentence on which the hearing turns is 'Simulations should be used as frequently as possible in all English classes from the third year of English teaching onwards.'

It would have been easy to fill in the gaps and remove ambiguities. The teachers' cards, while concentrating on school conditions, could also have had a definition of a simulation, and the inspectors' cards could have gone into the problems of Blue School. Instead of 'simulations should be used' I could have written 'must be used' or alternatively 'We recommend that simulations be used.' Instead of 'as frequently as possible' I could have been explicit and written 'at least once a week', or else specified who decides what is possible.

These five examples will give you some ideas of what I mean by an excluded middle. So if your simulation does not have one, consider whether it should be given one. I admit that it does take courage, and probably requires experience, deliberately to introduce holes. You may be worried that the participants will flounder around not knowing what to do. It is safer to spell everything out, but the result tends to be unimaginative and routine, verging on a guided exercise. Fortunately, most teachers who use simulations soon discover that the participants are not so helpless as some people assume, and that, given the power and the opportunity, not only cope with the difficulties, but prefer to take the chance of floundering rather than be spoon-fed with all the options.

Motives, interest and involvement

When rewriting it is useful to consider the motives of the participants. Why are they doing certain things? Are the thoughts going through their heads external to the event (to learn, to pass examinations, to please the teacher), or internal to the event (motivated by their roles and the problem)?

I use motive, motivated and motivation in the way these words might be used in a detective story rather than in a manual on physics. Educationalists tend to think of motivation as a synonym for keenness, using the word to mean motive power. They might remark, 'The students did not have much motivation,' in much the same way as they might say, 'The engine did not have much steam.'

This is not particularly helpful when rewriting simulations, as there is a fairly clear distinction between keenness on the one hand and motives on the other. For example, in some simulations participants may be motivated to speak in public because they have the job of radio announcer, or because they wish to protest against the injustice of the system, yet they can be far from keen to do this, and may be nervous and apprehensive. But although they lack motivation in the sense of keenness, this is overcome by the motives of duty, anger, responsibility, helpfulness, danger, co-operation or personal honour.

Motives (as distinct from keenness) are crucial in simulation design, and that is why I like facsimile documents rather than role cards and instructions, since they are more likely to awaken the motives of duty and responsibility on a personal level within the simulated environment. Often role cards are necessary or desirable, but in that case I prefer it when they refer to 'I', not 'You'. I feel that the participants are likely to accept their roles more easily if the card says 'My name is . . .' rather than 'Your name is . . .'

So if, during the run-through, there seemed to be a lack of interest at first and an overlong time before the participants became really involved, then re-examine the role cards.

The facsimile documents might also be rewritten to contain a greater sense of duty, danger, injustice or urgency. They might be rewritten to include threats or inducements ranging from 'As you know, the company's policy on promoting staff depends largely on the candidates' negotiating skills' to 'Any wilful disobedience of Space Orders will be dealt with by military tribunal.'

In simulations, the words 'interest' and 'involvement' are closely connected. Often participants are interested because they are involved, not because of the subject matter as such. A simulation does not become an interesting simulation because it is about an 'interesting' subject; such a simulation might be complicated, muddled and difficult to run. But a simulation about what might be thought of as a dull subject could be highly involving, and therefore highly interesting.

Naturally, the subject matter of your own simulations will probably be determined by the subject area in which you teach. But within that area you do not have to head straight for the 'interesting' bits, and when you come to rewriting the simulation it does not follow that you can make the event more interesting by throwing in more interesting facts.

As mentioned at the beginning of this chapter, when rewriting your simulations it is a good idea to start by looking at the whole event rather than concentrating on individual facts or documents. Remember that in simulations the interest and involvement are linked to the motives, and the motives are linked to functions – who the participants are, and what they have to do, and what they have to do it with.

· 6 · Writing the organizer's notes

Feedback and friendliness

Organizer's notes are likely to be useful for other teachers, and the effort of writing them is a discipline which will sharpen your understanding of your own simulation. But writing the notes is not easy and is often done badly. One of the main problems is that you know your simulation so well it is difficult to describe it objectively.

However, an early difficulty is what to call the person who runs the event, and thus what to call the notes used by that person. Most authors avoid the word 'teacher' so as not to give the impression that a simulation is a taught event. The traditional name is 'controller' and I used to draw an analogy with traffic controllers who help the flow of traffic but do not tell individual motorists which way to go. But this is still not satisfactory, and I switched to 'organizer', which is being adopted more often and is somewhat more neutral. But you can search for your own word – perhaps 'facilitator' might be better.

If you have written and tried out your own simulation and now want other people to use it without your supervision, you must incorporate into the organizer's notes the feedback from what happened in the classroom, feedback being a combination of your own observations plus the comments of the participants. Feedback helps in dealing with questions about practicalities – what does the organizer do if there are ten participants, or twenty, or thirty? How should the room space be organized? How long is the event likely to last? In what order should the documents be handed out? What useful points could be made during the briefing and the debriefing?

You can also use feedback for making specific points about possible or probable events during the action. This sort of feedback arises from chance remarks, initiatives, mistakes, doubts and comments made by participants. This is where a good memory (or tapes or notes) comes in handy. Honesty is also important. It is all too easy not to remember the occasions when things did not work out well, and it is often these sort of danger areas which the simulation-user wants signposted.

Most organizer's notes leave a lot to be desired. Sometimes they are little more than an expanded blurb, setting out a list of laudable aims and objectives. Sometimes these aims are at odds with the mechanism of the simulation. With most organizer's notes, there is no explanation of the nature of the simulation technique, and it is often referred to as a game or exercise, or else described in words borrowed from the theatre. The procedures for running the simulation are often described in vague generalities, and there is an impression that nothing ever goes wrong. Yet an inspection of the documents can raise all sorts of fundamental questions about how the simulation should be organized. In many notes the skimpiness of the treatment of the mechanics is followed by a long list of points to raise in the debriefing, implying that the simulation itself is of minor importance and that the only thing that really matters is whether or not the participants learn the subject matter.

Some notes are written as though they were articles about teaching the facts of a particular subject. But most of the users will probably know these facts already; what they need is information about the simulation. If you are writing for teachers of geography, history or science, you do not have to give a lecture about the facts of the subject and how important it is that the students should understand them. The teachers will know this. It is better to concentrate on the specific problem, the specific roles, documents and mechanics.

If you have written your simulation in the context of teaching English as a foreign language, there is no need to emphasize the importance of language and communication skills. It is more helpful to explain how your simulation works and how the technique can be used to provoke the students to talk spontaneously.

Another common fault in the notes is a surfeit of educational jargon. The user may be unfamiliar with simulations and may require friendly reassurance linked with examples of what to do, and also what not to do. All too often the notes seem to be written for academics, not for practising teachers. Instead of advice about what the organizer can do if one group finishes long before the other groups, there are generalizations, fashionable slogans, pseudo-scientific terminology, and sometimes just old-fashioned pomposity. Here are some actual examples from American simulation literature:

> To help participants develop empathy by experiencing the roles of those with value orientations and constraints different from their own.

> Technology/assessment impact evaluation to explore the secondary and tertiary outcomes that might be potential areas of impact.

> Information gathering and survey research to query participants for their pragmatic reactions to non-quantifiable data.

> Explore or estimate the probabilities that hypothetical events or trends are likely to happen through using opinions of experts in several rounds of consensus building.

Contrast the above with the following example from the organizer's notes to 'Bafa Bafa', in which Garry Shirts discusses the question of what happens in the debriefing if participants object to having been instructed that when visiting the other culture they should not ask about the rules of that culture.

'If I could have asked about the rules, I would have been able to do O.K. in the other culture', is the way belief may be expressed. Maybe, but asking questions in the simulation may be less like the 'real world' than one would think. Often members of the other culture speak a language or a dialect the visitor doesn't understand and so it is difficult to ask or answer questions. Moreover, we are often reluctant to ask questions about ways of behaving for fear of being rude. It's hard to ask why one does something without seeming to question the validity of that behaviour. Furthermore, many actions which are culturally determined are not evident to the person in the culture. Few Americans, for instance, are aware that they space themselves approximately 18 inches apart when standing in a group, or the conditions and circumstances which govern the amount of time it is appropriate for them to look another person directly in the eye.

The above example illustrates my point that the notes do not have to avoid awkward questions, and that they can be friendly. Potential users are likely to be reassured by Shirts's notes, feeling that they were written by an author who has tried out the simulation on many occasions, and who is well aware of the practical problems and the links between the simulation and the real world. And implicit in the remarks is the importance of people and the way they think, rather than seeing people as building bricks in the construction of a model.

Inconsistencies are a hazard when writing the notes. We have seen examples of inconsistencies in the documents and role cards (e.g. the married woman being labelled 'Miss') and this kind of mistake also occurs in the organizer's notes, perhaps to an even greater extent. The notes are sometimes written months after the completion of the other documents, and the author has forgotten that document A no longer mentions event Y, that the artifacts mentioned in document B were renamed, and that document C was eliminated altogether.

It is not unknown for the notes of published simulations to

refer to the handing out of a document that no longer exists, or not to mention a new document, or to have overlooked the fact that changes made to particular documents have affected the mechanics of the simulation.

I find that I have a confusion gap which starts about one week after completing the simulation. I can usually avoid inconsistencies if I either write the notes immediately on completing the documents or else forget about the project and come back to it after a couple of months and then conscientiously reread all of it.

Formats

There is no 'best' method of how to present information in the organizer's notes. It is largely a matter of personal preference. There is no particular order in which the facts of the simulation should be given, nor is there any format which is ideal for all simulations. Clearly, the presentation should be consistent with the particular simulation. If it has a 'hidden agenda' in which surprises are built in, this can be explained fairly early in the notes. If special technology is required, or extra room space, or if the simulation needs an especially large number of participants, this should be made clear at the start of the notes, not tucked away towards the end.

If you link several simulations together, there are more options available to you when writing the notes. You could have one booklet for the whole series, or write one booklet for each simulation. If you have individual notes for each simulation, you can restrict the information to the mechanics of that event, and link this with a general introduction which could be published on the inside cover of all of the simulations.

The individual notes in my 'Nine Graded Simulations' all have the same format, and this may suggest ways for organizing your own notes:

Contents

Time needed

Number of participants

A brief summary
Before class
Briefing
Action
Debriefing

The contents section is just a list of the documents. The time needed can vary, depending on the particular conditions in which the simulation is run and whether it is a full version or a short version. The number of participants takes into account the way they might be grouped. The brief summary explains who the participants are and the problem they face. The section entitled 'Before class' deals with organizing the documents and equipment that will be required. Briefing covers the handing out of notes for participants, setting time limits, etc. The information about the action varies considerably according to the simulation, and the final section on the debriefing mentions several avenues which could be explored in the discussion afterwards.

Each of the nine simulations incorporates the same general introduction which deals firstly with the simulation technique ('Simulations cannot be taught, for there is no teacher in the desert or newsroom'), and secondly with advice to the organizer which applies to any simulation ('When students become familiar with simulations, consider asking them to do some of the organizing').

If you have written several simulations, the writing of the notes is a good opportunity to think about whether these simulations could be linked as a series. Even if they are very different from each other, you could still consider linking them because they are different, thus providing a variety of roles, problems and environments.

If you can produce a series of simulations, important advantages accrue:

1. A series helps teachers and students who are unfamiliar with the simulation technique, since the first simulation is

usually the most difficult one, and after that the participants know what to expect.

2. By having several simulations together, both teachers and students can transfer skills, knowledge and organizational points from one event to another. If the organization of a committee in the first simulation (always speak to the chair, motions must have both proposer and seconder) works out well, the procedures adopted could be used in subsequent committee-type simulations.

3. A series of simulations provides a basis for comparison. This applies not only to assessing the value of the individual simulations, but to evaluating the behaviour of individual participants. With a series it is possible to see developmental benefits occurring because participants learn lessons from the previous event.

Whether you write the organizer's notes for an individual simulation or a series, you should remember that the user cannot read your mind. Various aspects of organization and procedure may seem self-evident to you because you are so familiar with them. But it might have been a long time since you first worked out these arrangements, and you have forgotten that they were not self-evident at the time.

If it is possible, watch someone else run your own simulation without any help apart from the notes. Don't interfere, don't give advice, just see what happens. As a result of this experience you may well find it necessary to clarify the instructions.

One possibility, for example, is to include diagrams of the layout of classroom furniture. The following diagrams are taken from Vernon's 'Talking Rocks', and my 'We're Not Going to Use Simulations'. You may think that these particular diagrams are too self-evident to be included, and you could be right. But on the other hand it is often better to err on the side of over-simplicity for at least a few organizational details. This not only avoids forcing the user to make an agonizing number of organizational decisions, but also reassures teachers that the simulation really does work.

The action – stage 1

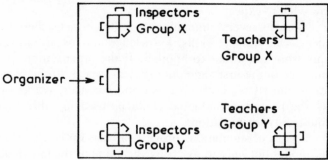

The action – stage 2

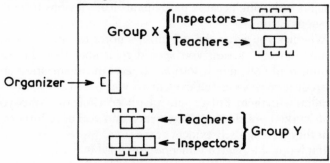

The debriefing

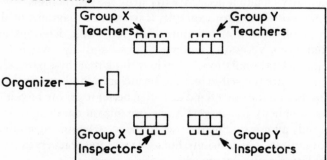

Suggested room arrangements for 'We're Not Going to Use Simulations'

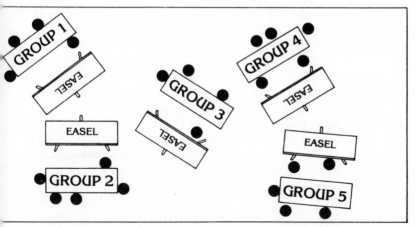

Suggested room arrangement for 'Talking Rocks'

Aims, achievements and assessment

Aims are not achievements, but many simulations have notes which seem to confuse the two. Most organizer's notes start with a section on 'Aims and objectives' (what's the difference?), and although this can give the user an idea of what went through the author's mind in designing the simulation, it says nothing about the probability of such aims being achieved.

My own advice is to see what the simulation achieves, and then write these up as the aims. After all, you are not engaged in academic research, you are trying to help teachers run a simulation. The advantages of this procedure are that:

1 the aims will probably be achieved, since the achievements occurred in the test runs;
2 some achievements which were not originally envisaged may have occurred, and these can be incorporated into the aims;
3 the concentration on experience rather than aims will assist you in presenting a clear account of what teachers can expect to happen when running your simulation.

Examples of a disjunction between aims and achievements are not hard to find. The Teacher's Guide to 'North Sea Challenge' states that the three simulations have one main aim – 'to enable students to participate in the experience of decision-making'. Yet the key decision on whether the construction site should be at Stomar or Inverlochen has been made by the author. The oil company representatives are instructed to announce half-way through a public meeting that the choice is Inverlochen, and that's that. The meeting is allowed to debate this decision but has no powers to change it.

A classic example of the opposite case – limited aims and large achievements – concerns the simulation 'Humanus', by P. A. Twelker and K. Layden, which was written for courses on futurology. Probably less than one 'Humanus' user in a thousand is engaged in futurology. Most teachers use the simulation because of its social, ethical and political achievements. The environment of the nuclear fallout shelter profoundly affects the participants emotionally, and what actually happens in their minds and in their behaviour is an achievement far greater than the limited aim of producing an experience as a basis for an academic discussion about the future.

By achievements, I do not mean merely the end result. Often the outcome is far less important than the process of reaching the result, and it is within the course of the action that valuable achievements may be discerned.

If you have written a good and fully participatory simulation on rivers in Africa, you are being far too restricted if you simply write, 'The aim is to give the students a better understanding of rivers in Africa.' If you want to have a section on aims, talk to the participants and the class teacher after the test run.

Sometimes you may not be present during the test run and will have to rely on the reports of the class teacher. I have never found that written reports are very satisfactory. My experience is that most teachers give generalizations and conclusions, rather than describe how they introduced the simulation, how long it took, and so on. Even if they are enthusiastic about what happened, the details are usually lacking.

The following example is taken from the transcript of a taped interview (not my own) with a teacher who had just run a simulation about the media:

There are about twenty-two in the class and they are poorly motivated, or they are academically limited, or they have caused some sort of behaviour problems. This particular class was very apathetic, very dead, very fed up with themselves and all their teaching. I thought this simulation would be a good thing to get them going, get them stirred up a bit. I'm not sure what specifically I was hoping for but I think the success was in the way they were working during the two double periods – they were working much harder than I thought they were capable of, and they were very involved in what they were doing. They were working with each other in a way I've never seen them doing before, working to improve each other's terminology, and their spelling as well. Also, because they were motivated as groups, fairly able children had a chance to show their ability without being seen to work.

This teacher is not very specific about what went on in the classroom but it is clear that the achievement lay in the behaviour, rather than in the learning of facts about media studies. Also the teacher referred to the participants working to improve each other's terminology and spelling, and such observations are worth considering when writing the organizer's notes.

If you include a section on assessment in the organizer's notes, there is no need to feel that subjective assessment of behaviour is in some way inferior to objective assessment of knowledge. On the contrary, an effective assessment of most non-material things that are of value in this world can be done only subjectively, and cannot be added up on a pocket calculator.

· 7 · Conclusions

The technique and the philosophy

Simulation is not just another educational technique. It is accompanied by a philosophy, and simulations are sufficiently distinctive from games, case studies and drama to merit their own unique place in educational theory.

The last four chapters have delved into simulation design, and it is now easier to move forward from the theoretical discussion in chapter 1, which raised objections to both the assembly-line approach and the definition that a simulation imitated reality.

An important clarification is the distinction between the materials and the event. Both are called simulations, but in an educational context it is the event which is the essence; it is the thoughts and behaviour of the participants which should be the focus of attention when thinking about definitions and about philosophy.

In the preceding chapters, example after example occurred which pointed to the importance of the author distinguishing between simulations and other techniques, a key factor being that a simulation is not a taught event. Embodied within this condition is the educational philosophy that learners should be (for at least some of the time) active participants in the learning process. And the simulation technique takes this philosophy one stage further: not only should there be occasions when learners should be active, there should also be occasions when they are in charge of events and have full authority, responsibility and function.

Once one grants that a simulation is about people and autonomy, rather than models, then human values emerge. Anyone who has had experience in running simulations knows that all sorts of behaviour can occur: honesty and dishonesty, tolerance and intolerance, altruism and selfishness, integrity and deceit, pride and envy, respect and disrespect, conscientiousness and indifference, formality and informality, seriousness and humour.

But whatever the individual values, there is an overriding philosophical concept implicit in treating learners as human beings who are in charge of events. To grant power and responsibility is itself a philosophical event, an act of politics involving government. Even if no words are stated, it is a transfer of power, a token of respect, an appeal for honour and consent, a gift of democracy, and a request for the acceptance of duties and responsibilities. A simulation is not just another educational technique.

Changes in values

In a pamphlet 'English from 5 to 16' written by Her Majesty's Inspectors, there are lists of objectives. Most pupils, it says, should at the age of 16 be able to 'Explain clearly a process of some complexity. . . . Argue a case. . . . Be aware of the need to match the way one speaks to the purpose, context and audience; and to be able to do so in a range of situations, social and otherwise.'

Unfortunately, the pupils in most secondary schools are given no opportunity to do these things. In most classrooms, the only person who explains a process of some complexity or argues a case is the teacher. In most classrooms the range of situations is extremely limited, and is dominated by dictatorial teaching.

The consequence is inescapable – most students have never had to organize themselves, argue a case, explain processes or be in charge of events, and when they are placed in such a position in further or higher education, or in any situation outside the educational field, they tend to be bad at it, and no wonder. In the secondary-school classroom the atmosphere should be safe, in which pupils are free of anxiety about making mistakes. But usually it is fraught with the anxiety of finding the right answer and avoiding being corrected, ticked off or humiliated by the teacher.

This behaviour gets carried over into their first simulation, and may become intensified since no 'right answer' may be apparent. So newcomers to simulations often try to escape by grabbing the first quick answer that comes to mind, or by play-acting, or playing the fool, rather than accepting power and responsibility. If their first simulation is a committee event and the person in the chair opens the discussion by looking across the table and saying 'Well, what do you think of X idea?', the reaction is often an embarrassed silence as the participant grabs for a document and starts looking for 'the' answer. This is not natural behaviour. It is secondary-school behaviour, and is a learned response to a particular type of teaching.

In primary school, on the other hand, children are in charge of a fairly wide range of events, and explore options. They function, and engage in genuine simulations, with a variety of materials – sand, water, tokens of exchange, shopping goods, paints, clothes, building materials – and engage in architecture, business, construction, aesthetic decisions, invention, adaptation and so on. In doing so, they are functioning as professionals rather than as pupils. But not in secondary school. When they leave secondary school, the damaging effects of dictatorial teaching diminishes but in some people never completely vanishes. One consequence of such teaching is that it is easier to use simulations with infants or adults than it is with teenagers.

Obviously, there are honourable exceptions, and there are many secondary schools and teachers who accept the philosophy of pupil participation and power, and use appropriate techniques. And clearly, the Inspectorate and other organizations are now arguing for a move away from teacher domination. This has already occurred in the field of English as a foreign language (EFL), where what is usually called the Communicative Movement has made important inroads into the former dictatorial methods based on teaching vocabulary, grammar and pronunciation. What is now stressed is that language should be used to communicate, and in EFL the change in philosophy and methods go hand in hand.

Towards an acceptable definition

One reason why the technique of simulations is so often separated from the philosophy is that the wrong words are used. We have already seen in chapter 1 that both ISAGA and SAGSET define a simulation as 'A working representation of reality', which suggests the model-making shop or the toy department. The definitions given in dictionaries use words like 'feign, pretend, imitation, assume falsely the appearance of . . .' and academics have followed the same line of thought. The words 'model, system, representation, artificial, substitute' occur frequently. Here are two examples of what they say about a simulation:

> Delineates a range of dynamic representations which employ substitute elements to replace real world components. (Taylor and Carter 1970)

> A simulation is the all-inclusive term which contains those activities which produce artificial environments or which provide artificial experiences for the participants in the activity. (Garvey 1971)

As we have seen, there is a significant difference between the environment which is simulated and the behaviour which is real. The academic definition fails to make this distinction.

We have also seen that a simulation cannot be a taught event:

the two are contradictions in terms. If it is taught, it is an event which requires a different label. Again, the academic definition misses the crux of the matter. It says nothing about reality of function, a reality which must include power and responsibility, obligations and duties. Models and representations, on the other hand, can be taught, and are often taught by dictatorial methods. By using the language of the construction industry, the academic definition fails to alert the reader to what happens in simulations.

The definition makes it difficult for a teacher to run a simulation, and both the definition and the assembly-line theory make it difficult to design a simulation. Together, they present a completely misleading account of simulations, and consequently impede the natural link between the technique and the philosophy.

My own definition of simulations has gradually evolved over the years. In my first book (Jones 1980) I criticized existing definitions and expressed a preference for descriptions. But I added, 'If a short definition is really necessary, perhaps it might be "Simulations are reality." From the teacher's point of view at least it errs on the right side, the side of function, the side of presenting good simulations and avoiding poor ones.'

In my second book (Jones 1982b) I devised the following definition of an educational simulation:

Reality of function in a simulated and structured environment.

This definition is still brief, but it now distinguishes between the behaviour and the environment. I used the word 'structured' to point out one of the differences between a simulation and episodic role-play. The phrase 'reality of function' helps to show that a simulation is not the same as play-acting or gaming. And since the function has to be real, the simulation cannot be an event occurring under the dictation of a teacher. Today I might ask for a little more space, and say something like:

A simulation in education is an untaught event in which sufficient information is provided to allow the participants to achieve reality of function in a simulated environment.

Harmonizing the concepts

Once the definition matches the activity, and the unfortunate recommendation of sequential authorship is removed, the concept of simulations becomes remarkably simple, yet highly effective. It is child-like (not childish) and sophisticated.

Stripped of all the misleading words about 'game', 'model' and 'representation', the concept has a unity of activity and aim. It is a concept which links the design, the action and the philosophy. There is an interaction between these three aspects which is satisfyingly straightforward and uncomplicated.

The design is a commonsense affair, tasting and mixing, adjusting and readjusting, in the light of the philosophy of participant power. The action itself is likely to be straightforward and without complicated intrusions by non-simulation techniques and terminology. And the philosophy can be developed and strengthened by both the thoughts of authorship and the behaviour of participants.

As you design simulations you will surely find that an appreciation of the philosophy is of practical help in the authorship, action and assessment.

The purpose of this book has been to encourage you to create your own simulations. If you do so, I wish you all possible success. I hope that you have already started. The essence of a simulation is action, and the virtue of doing rather than observing is summed up in the old Chinese proverb:

I hear and I forget,
I see and I remember,
I do and I understand.

References and further reading

Simulations

'African Village Development Game', Cathy S. Greenblat (unpublished).

'Bafa Bafa', Garry Shirts (1977), Del Mar, California, Simile II.

'Blood Money', Cathy S. Greenblat and John Gagnon (1975), Bethesda, Maryland, National Heart, Lung and Blood Institute, OPCE.

'Five Simple Business Games' ('Gorgeous Gateaux Ltd', 'Fresh Oven Pies Ltd', 'Dart Aviation Ltd', 'The Island Game', 'The Republic Game'), Charles Townsend (1978), Cambridge, CRAC publications/Hobsons Press.

'Fort', Ken Jones (unpublished).

'Greenwood Gypsy Site', Gordon Cooper (1984), London, Community Service Volunteers, 237 Pentonville Road, N1.

'Humanus', P. A. Twelker and K. Layden, Del Mar, California, Simile II.

'Linguan Prize for Literature, The', Ken Jones (unpublished, but see Ken Jones (1985) 'The Linguan Prize for Literature' in *Perspectives on Gaming and Simulation 10*, Loughborough, SAGSET).

'Man in His Environment' (1971), London, Coca-Cola Export Corporation.

'Mary Rose, The', Aylesbury, Ginn.

'Nine Graded Simulations' ('Survival', 'Front Page', 'Radio Coving-ham', 'Property Trial', 'Appointments Board', 'The Dolphin Pro-ject', 'Airport Controversy', 'The Azim Crisis', 'Action for Libel'), Ken Jones (1984), Munich, Max Hueber. Also available from Basil Blackwell, Oxford, as 'Graded Simulations' (1985). Originally published by ILEA in 1974.

'North Sea Challenge' ('Strike', 'Slick', 'Impact'), Michael Lynch (1979), London, BP Educational Service.

'Running the British Economy 1984', Keith Lumsden and Alex Scott (1984), London, Longman Micro Software.

'Sixgam' (1984), London, Pitmansoft.

'Spring Green Motorway', Stephen Joseph, Nick Lester and CSV (1980), London, Community Service Volunteers, 237 Pentonville Road, N1.

'Starpower', Garry Shirts (1969), Del Mar, California, Simile II.

'Talking Rocks', R. F. Vernon (1978), Del Mar, California, Simile II.

'Tenement' (1980), London, Shelter, 157 Waterloo Road, SE1.

'Terry Parker', Nigel Gann (1975), London, Community Service Volunteers, 237 Pentonville Road, N1.

'We're Not Going to Use Simulations', Ken Jones (1982), in *Simulations in Language Teaching*, Cambridge, Cambridge University Press.

'Year of the Dove', Ken Jones (unpublished).

References

Department of Education and Science, HMI Series (1984) *English from 5 to 16*, London, HMSO.

Duke, R. D. (1979a) 'Format for the game – logic or intuition?', in *How to Build a Simulation/Game*, the Proceedings of the Tenth ISAGA Conference, Leeuwarden, the Netherlands, vol. 1, 59–67.

Duke, R. D. (1979b) 'Nine steps to game design', in *How to Build a Simulation/Game*, the Proceedings of the Tenth ISAGA Conference, Leeuwarden, the Netherlands, vol. 1, 98–112.

Ellington, H., Addinall, E. and Percival, F. (1982) *A Handbook of Game Design*, London, Kogan Page.

Garvey, M. D. (1971) 'Simulations, a catalogue of judgements, findings and hunches', in Tansey, P. J. (ed.) *Educational Aspects of Simulations*, London, McGraw-Hill.

Greenblat, C. S. and Duke, R. D. (1982) *Principles and Practices of*

Gaming-Simulation, Beverly Hills, California, and London, Sage Publications.

Jones, K. (1974) 'From Shelter – a simulation', Games & Puzzles, 25, 14–16.

Jones, K. (1980) *Simulations: A Handbook for Teachers*, London, Kogan Page.

Jones, K. (1981) 'Introducing Simulations', *Practical English Teaching*, 1 (4), 15–16.

Jones, K. (1982a) 'Simulations as Examinations', *Simulation/Games for Learning*, 12 (1) 3–13.

Jones, K. (1982b) *Simulations in Language Teaching*, Cambridge, Cambridge University Press.

Shirts, R. G. (1975) 'Ten mistakes commonly made by persons designing educational simulations and games', *SAGSET Journal*, 5 (4), 147–50.

Taylor, J. L. and Carter, K. R. (1970) 'A decade of instructional simulation in urban and regional studies', in Armstrong, R. H. R. and Taylor, J. L. (eds) *Instructional Simulation Systems in Higher Education*, Cambridge, Cambridge Institute of Education.

Walford, R. A. (1983) 'Spring Green Motorway: A question of reconstruction', *Simulation/Games for Learning*, 13 (4), 156–65.

Further reading

I know of no other book devoted exclusively to the design of simulations, but there are books involving the design of games, simulations, role-play, exercises, etc. There are also books on simulations which have sections dealing with design. For further reading, the following books may be useful:

Boocock, S. S. and Schild, E. O. (eds) (1968) *Simulation Games in Learning*, Beverly Hills, California, Sage Publications.

Davidson, A. and Gordon, P. (1978) *Games and Simulations in Action*, London, Woburn Press.

Duke, R. D. (1974) *Gaming: The Future's Language*, New York, Wiley.

Gibbs, G. I. (ed.) (1974) *Handbook of Games and Simulation Exercises*, London, E. and F. N. Spon.

Horn, R. E. and Cleaves, A. (1980) *The Guide to Simulation Games for Education and Training*, 4th edn, Beverly Hills, California, Sage Publication.

Pfeiffer, J. W. and Jones, J. E. (1979) *A Handbook of Structured Experiences for Human Relations Training*, vols 1–7, La Jolla, California, University Associates.

Tansey, P. J. (ed.) (1971) *Educational Aspects of Simulations*, London, McGraw-Hill.

Taylor, J. L. and Walford, R. (1978) *Learning and the Simulation Game*, Milton Keynes, Open University Press.

Van Ments, M. (1983) *The Effective Use of Role-Play: A Handbook for Teachers and Trainers*, London, Kogan Page.

Journals and societies

SAGSET, the Society for the Advancement of Games and Simulations in Education and Training, is the leading society in Europe devoted to the encouragement of those who use simulations and games. The Society's journal, *Simulations/Games for Learning* (formerly *SAGSET Journal*), is a quarterly and includes *SAGSET News*. SAGSET runs an annual conference and publishes the proceedings under the general title *Perspectives on Gaming and Simulation*. Details may be obtained from: The Secretary, SAGSET, Centre for Extension Studies, University of Technology, Loughborough, Leicestershire, LE11 3TU.

Simulation and Games is the official publication of the North American Simulation and Gaming Association (NASAGA), the International Simulation and Gaming Association (ISAGA) and the Association for Business Simulation and Experiential Learning (ABSEL). It is a quarterly, available from Sage Publications, Beverly Hills, California, and London.

ISAGA Newsletter. This publication is available to ISAGA members only and usually contains information about courses, conferences and publications, plus occasional articles.

Simjeux/Simgames. A Canadian quarterly available from Pierre Corbeil, 690, 104c Avenue, Drummondville, Quebec, J2B 49P.

Index